LENGTHE
SHADOWS

Bletchley and Woburn Sands district
& the impact of Milton Keynes
1970–2003

Ted Enever

The
Book
Castle

For Mark and Rachel

Also by Ted Enever:
Cockney Kid and Countrymen: The second World War
remembered by the children of Woburn Sands and Aspley Guise.
Changing Faces, Changing Places: Bletchley and Woburn Sands
district 1945–1970.
Britain's Best Kept Secret – Ultra's base at Bletchley Park.

First published November 2003 by
The Book Castle
12 Church Street
Dunstable
Bedfordshire LU5 4RU

ISBN 1 903747 43 0

Printed by Antony Rowe Ltd., Chippenham, Wiltshire

Front Cover:
Top: Jazz legend, John Dankworth.
Main picture: Moore Place, Aspley Guise, after its 1980s refurbishment.
Bottom: Taking the strain at a Bow Brickhill show.

Back Cover:
Top: Author Ted Enever in deputy sheriff's uniform.
Middle: Bletchley's new leisure centre takes shape in the early 1970s.
*Bottom: Woburn Sands Phoenix Club members with their stall at a Christmas
lights switch on.*

ACKNOWLEDGMENTS

As I complete this trilogy relating to life in Aspley Guise, Woburn Sands, Bow Brickhill, Bletchley and Fenny Stratford, I cannot thank enough the many people now living in, or connected with those areas, regarding the help they have given me in putting these three books together.

In relation to this current work, 'Lengthening Shadows', I must pay tribute to the assistance given me by the following: Betty Abbott, Bruce Abbott, Ron Beacham, Ray Bellchambers, Robin Bowen-Williams, Jack Bromfield, Enid Burton, Eileen Cordon, Bill and Ann Cox, Mike Dickins, Roly Doggett, Stan Green, Lionel Grech, Gordon Hart, John Hill, Tim Hill, Vivien Hoare, Odette Holland, Leslie Holliman, Trevor Johnson, Michael Kemp, Steve Larner, Douglas and Christine Loak, Ken Meadley, Les Nunn, Bob Page, Guin Parker, David Parkins, Alroy Pickersgill, Ernest Pye, Barbara Smith, Lyn Stapleton, Tracy Whitmore, Roger Wyatt and Mary Yates. In addition, many other people have telephoned with snippets of information or suggestions as to where I might find answers to questions, so if any of these are not named above forgive me, but you have not been forgotten and I am very grateful for your help and interest. Last, but by no means least, to Karoline at Office World in Milton Keynes for her patience and understanding in getting photos and illustrations copied to my satisfaction.

Writing any book is not the easy task many people imagine and the last three months have gradually grown more hectic as my editorial deadline drew closer. Suffering my lack of interest in anything not to do with this text has been my family, and as I know I have tried their patience on many occasions during the past weeks, thank you for putting up with me.

In conclusion, I am grateful to Paul Bowes, my publisher, and to Sally Siddons, the Book Castle's publishing manager, for having the confidence in my ability to write for them.

Thank you, each and everyone.

About the author....

Ted Enever was educated at Bedford Modern School and entered journalism in 1951 with the Bletchley District Gazette. After his two years National Service in the army he continued his career as a freelance, combining this with work in the family greengrocery business. He returned to staff journalism in 1964. In 1967 he became editor of the Bucks Standard at Newport Pagnell before joining Marshall Cavendish, the London based international publishers, as deputy managing editor. In 1971 Mr Enever joined the Inner London Education Authority as managing editor, and publications which he launched and controlled won many national trade awards. In 1987 he was appointed Director of Public Affairs with the British Dental Association before joining Milton Keynes Development Corporation, two years later, where he managed all media relations and was involved in a wide range of marketing, ceremonial and public relations activities.

Retiring when the Corporation was wound up in 1992, Ted Enever was a founder member of the Bletchley Park Trust and served as its chief executive and a trustee in its formative years. He still plays an active part in the Trust's fund-raising activities and is author of a successful book detailing the setting up of the wartime code-breaking centre, 'Britain's Best Kept Secret – Ultra's Base at Bletchley Park'. He was recently made a patron of the Bletchley Park Trust.

A keen gardener and sportsman, Ted Enever is a past president of Bletchley St Martin's Bowls Club. Married with two children, Ted, wife Barbara and daughter Rachel now live in Bletchley after having homes in Bow Brickhill for many years. Ted's son, Mark, still lives in the village. Recently the family extended its interest in racing by becoming co-owners of two horses, both trained by Peter Harris at his stables in Tring.

CONTENTS

INTRODUCTION

When I sat down to write 'Cockney Kid and Countrymen', the first book in this trilogy, I had little idea that it would lead on to two more books covering my own memories of life, and those of others who live in that corridor of land covering Bletchley and Fenny Stratford, Bow Brickhill, Woburn Sands and, just across the border into Bedfordshire, Aspley Guise.

From those early Second World War days when I was a child in Aspley Guise, through the post war years leading up to the emergence of Milton Keynes – covered in the second book 'Changing Faces, Changing Places' – and now in this text, 'Lengthening Shadows', the people of this area have witnessed the most phenomenal social and physical changes. Within this book, covering the period from 1970 to the present day, I have examined Bletchley's boom years of the early 1970s, looked at its rapid decline during the 1980s, its failed attempts at regeneration in the late 1990s, and give some positive pointers, I hope, to its plans for the future.

Alongside this, I have not forgotten the villages, for their character, too, has changed enormously in the 30 or more years covered. What were almost self-supporting communities have now become little more than dormitories, though Woburn Sands has remained busy and is still set to expand.

I would stress at this point, however, that this book is not an academic history of the area, but an overview of events that have brought it to the position it is in today. It is, perhaps, a little more serious than its two predecessors – stronger on fact, maybe, and a little less anecdotal – and that thought leads me to its title. 'Lengthening Shadows' certainly gives a sense of the ever-increasing size of Milton Keynes, and particularly the importance of Central Milton Keynes now as a regional centre, and the influence that size has on the established communities that have been absorbed to make up the whole. But, as we get older, our own shadows of life lengthen and I have now spent 63 of my 69 years in and around Bletchley and Woburn Sands.

For those who have paid me the compliment of reading the first two books in this trilogy and who now embark on the last phase, I trust you will not be disappointed. For those new to my pen, I hope you will enjoy what you read and that it will stimulate your thoughts.

Now, I think I may have a rest; three books in three years isn't too bad, I submit, for a cockney kid who is now a countryman, who has seen many changing faces and changing places, but whose own shadows of life are beginning to lengthen... Let me sign off, if I may, with Shakespeare's words: 'I wish you all the joy that you can wish.'

Ted Enever – Bletchley, May 2003

An active interest in community affairs has gone hand in glove with author Ted Enever's career as a professional communicator. See page 143.

CHAPTER 1
BOOMING BLETCHLEY

As Great Britain said goodbye to the decade that was to become known as 'the swinging sixties' and welcomed the 1970s, North Bucks had known for nearly three years that it was to become home to the new city of Milton Keynes. The plans available at that time showed that the new city would take well in excess of some 20,000 acres of land for its overall development and encompass the existing towns of Wolverton and Stony Stratford, in the north, and Bletchley and Fenny Stratford in the south. Twelve rural parishes were also to be absorbed into the new development.

The initial announcement, made in 1967, that the city was to be built, provoked widespread opposition from the farming community and those with concerns for the rural environment. More importantly, perhaps, from the point of view of this part of my own story of life in North Bucks from 1940 onwards, was the fact that Bletchley, which had always imagined itself to be, and indeed wanted to be, the focal point of any major development, was to be merely one of six 'centres' which would go to make up the new Milton Keynes. With three new centres planned for Central Milton Keynes and on the east and west flanks at areas designated as Kingston and Westcroft respectively, the other three were to be the existing towns of Wolverton, Stony Stratford, and Bletchley alongside Fenny Stratford.

Bletchley had followed expansionist policies since the end of the Second World War in 1945, though the community had grown steadily for a hundred years previously when the main railway line, from London to Rugby, was routed to the south of what was then a small village close to the important township of Fenny Stratford. In the late 18th and early 19th centuries, Fenny Stratford, along with Stony Stratford some seven miles to the north, was a prosperous coaching town sitting astride the old Roman Watling Street. When the Grand Union canal was built at Fenny Stratford in 1800, the future of the place seemed assured.

But the railway, arriving in 1838, was to change that and from the mid-19th century onwards, Bletchley expanded towards Fenny Stratford until the two communities merged. By the time the world lurched into war in 1939, the town of Bletchley was becoming a serious rival to its older neighbour and was recognised as anything to the south of the railway line. The original village to the north of this point was now known as Old Bletchley but not until the rapid expansion of the town in the late 1940s and throughout the 1950s and 1960s, did Old Bletchley find itself subject to serious developmental pressures, as did the neighbouring parish of Water Eaton, to the south-west of Fenny Stratford.

For Old Bletchley those pressures meant the creation of what we know today as Far Bletchley, with housing development covering vast tracks of land from Denbigh Bridge on the Watling Street west to the Buckingham Road, and the wedge of land between this highway and the road to Newton Longville.

The body charged in 1967 with the implementation of the new city's development was the Milton Keynes Development Corporation, and the Corporation chose as the master plan for the new city that drawn up by consultants Llewellyn-Davies, Weekes, Forestier-Walker and Bor. This showed Milton Keynes to be a city served by a grid pattern of roads and with imaginative use of its water courses – the rivers, brooks and canal – as the backbone of its open spaces.

By 1970, the Corporation, or MKDC as it quickly became known, was well established in its headquarters at Wavendon Tower, ironically just yards outside the boundary, or designated area as it was then called, of the new city. Wavendon Tower was built in 1893 by Lieutenant-

Wavendon Tower pictured in the early years of its life.

Colonel Henry Burney, JP, just after the death of his father, who was Wavendon's rector. And, it seems, the picture gallery in the house boasted some excellent family portraits painted by Hogarth, Rembrandt and Gainsborough. It became the Corporation's base following Government asking Newport Pagnell Rural District Council if it knew of any suitable properties. At the time the RDC said that both Wavendon Tower and nearby Walton Hall were available.

In 1968, a year after the Corporation moved in to Wavendon Tower, the chairman of the Open University's planning committee visited Milton Keynes in his quest to find an out of London home for the organisation, set up some two years earlier and the brainchild of Labour's prime minister Harold Wilson. Lord Campbell of Eskan, the Labour peer who headed the Corporation's managing Board, was keen to have a higher education facility in Milton Keynes as soon as possible, and a meeting with Geoffrey Crowther – later Lord Crowther – the Open University treasurer, set the wheels in motion. By 1969 Walton Hall, the former residence of Brigadier Earle, a much respected man locally, was the Open University's new headquarters. Meanwhile, the

3

Members of the Board of Milton Keynes Development Corporation pictured outside Milton Keynes Community Centre following the first Board meeting on 15 June 1967. Left to right are Walter Ismay, A.Meikle, Lord Campbell, Lady Serota, Horace Cutler, Margaret Durbridge, Sir Ralph Verney, Ray Bellchambers.

additional staff needed to get Milton Keynes off the ground were pouring in to Wavendon Tower and it quickly became clear that extra space was needed here. New offices began to spring up in the grounds.

Lord 'Jock' Campbell's managing Board drew its membership from a wide range of disciplines. Local representation was vested in the late Jim Cassidy, the then chairman of Bletchley Urban District Council, who served alongside the late Mrs Margaret Durbridge, JP, of Newport Pagnell, who was a Bucks County Councillor, and Ray Bellchambers, a long serving member of Newport Pagnell Rural District Council and chairman of that council in 1965.

Ray Bellchambers now lives in Bancroft, in Milton Keynes and, at the age of 84, is the only surviving member of the original Board. He remembers well the disappointment shown by Jim Cassidy and his fellow Bletchley councillors of the time that their town was not to be the focal point of the city, though he also recalls how Bletchley, recognised for many years as the commercial and civic centre of North Bucks, might just have added to its growing reputation.

It came about, Ray told me, in a somewhat diverse way by future population figures for the South East of England being found to be way off the mark. By the late 1960s population movement in Britain – what the planners called 'the drift to the south' – had almost ceased, so instead of the south-east of England having an additional population by 1981 of some 3.5 million, the projected figure was revised to only 2.6 million.

Though the founding of Milton Keynes was never in doubt, this did raise questions as to the ultimate size of the city, and Peter Shore, then the minister responsible, came to Milton Keynes to discuss with the Board possible target reductions from 250,000 to 200,000 inhabitants. This was mooted in subsequent parliamentary discussions but never enforced. However, when these developments became known to Bletchley Council, it quickly but quietly – some would use the word secretly – began to put together its own development plan for Bletchley to expand to a town of some 70,000 people. Alongside this, the MKDC Board were working on an interim report, which included Bletchley, Stony Stratford and Wolverton being positively integrated into the whole scheme of things, and which would be part of the basis from which Milton Keynes would really begin. The initial strategy was to start at the city centre – Lloyds Court – but to develop the first roads to connect north and south, that is to say, the existing towns. The local Conservative MP Bill Benyon, who had deposed Labour's Bob Maxwell in the June 1970 general election, felt strongly enough to tell his constituents at the time that Milton Keynes, as planned, 'must go ahead'.

As is the way of things in local government planning, a public inquiry into the interim report was held at Bletchley's Wilton Hall in the same month that the general election took place. The inquiry was a lengthy affair, lasting some ten days, with among the major points of debate the siting of the city's new sewage works at Willen and the size of

Margaret Durbridge and Ray Bellchambers examine the construction of Milton Keynes' first main sewer which ran under Linford Wood.

development to be known as Central Milton Keynes. Certainly the arguments about the siting of the sewage works convinced the inspector to uphold these objections and the MKDC Board then opted for the present-day site of the works at Cotton Valley, next to the M1 motorway. All in all, though, the Development Corporation's Board got what it wanted; the go-ahead for Milton Keynes.

Ray Bellchambers was at the inquiry and remembers how Bletchley representatives suddenly introduced details of the Urban Council's plans to expand Bletchley to 70,000 as an individual entity. However, Robert Dunbabin, who lived at Sherington, was clerk to Ray's Newport Pagnell Rural District Council and a schoolboy chum of the young Bellchambers in the 1930s, knew the local government rule book by heart and tended to run his Council by it. He was quickly on his feet to point out to the Inspector that Bletchley was out of order in raising the matter. Bletchley's development ideas, he said, meant encroachment into

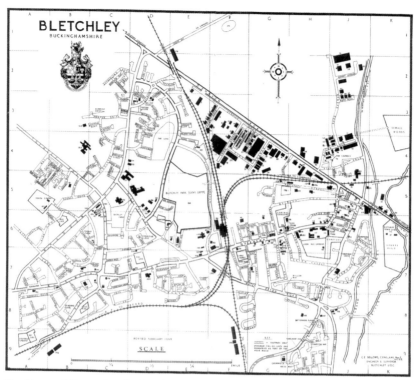

Bletchley and Fenny Stratford in the early 1970s. Note the lack of development north of the A5 Watling Street and to the north-west of Whaddon Way.

other local authority areas and no consultation had been held with these other authorities, of which Newport Pagnell Rural District Council was one. The Inspector noted his protest and the Bletchley representatives were refrained from putting their case.

With the inquiry behind them, Ray Bellchambers and his fellow Board members then began to hone the ideas of their planning consultants into the positive shapes of Milton Keynes that we know today. Within months Wavendon Tower could not accommodate its influx of staff, as I have mentioned above. Engineers and land valuers had joined the departments of chief engineer Ernest Pye and estates officer Alan Ashton, for all new towns start with land acquisition, roads and sewers. Architects were quick to follow, and with the penchant for many of these gentlemen to wear sombre, dark business clothes, were quickly christened 'the men in the black suits' by a still somewhat sceptical local population.

Ray Bellchambers was conscious of this public feeling, being a North Bucks man through and through. Born in New Bradwell in 1919, Ray served an apprenticeship in Wolverton Works, with part of his training being carried out in Derby where he worked on locomotives. When war came in 1939 he switched to working on the land and carried out a variety of tasks, including the dredging of local brooks and streams which in those days were often prone to flooding.

By the end of hostilities Ray was foreman at Wing agricultural depot, one of many such depots sited throughout the country to oversee land usage throughout the war and to keep machinery in good repair. However, his interest in matters political saw him as secretary of the Buckingham constituency Labour party at this time – virtually the whole of North Bucks was encompassed by the Buckingham constituency in those days – and he was given time off from work to steer Aiden Crawley home as the area's MP in the 1945 general election. After a year at Ruskin College, Oxford, in 1946, Ray had the necessary training behind him to become a full-time Labour party agent before attempting to become a parliamentary candidate for Chesterfield and Wycombe. Unsuccessful on both counts, Ray returned to Wolverton Works in 1948 and was elected to Newport Pagnell Rural District Council that year. He was to go on to complete some 25 years with that authority until local government changes in the early 1970s did away with Newport RDC, Newport UDC, Wolverton UDC and Bletchley UDC, these four authorities being replaced by a single Milton Keynes Borough Council.

For his services to the Milton Keynes area over the years, Ray was awarded the OBE in February 1980 and with Frank Atter, who served on Wolverton UDC for many years and was later to join the MKDC Board, was awarded alderman status by Milton Keynes Borough Council. Ray lost his wife, formerly Mary Turner, the daughter of a well-

The Fenny Stratford end of Bletchley showing the putting green and tennis courts of Central Gardens, bottom; the Studio cinema, centre; and Leon Avenue and Lennox Road, top. Bletchley Road runs across the centre of the picture.

known Old Bradwell nurseryman, in 1998 and the couple, married in 1942, had two sons. A founder member of Milton Keynes Museum, which has been on the scene now for more than thirty years, Ray is currently president of that organisation.

I remember well the first time Ray Bellchambers became known to me. Sitting in 1951 as a very new and very junior reporter in the tiny Bletchley District Gazette office in Central Gardens Approach, Bletchley, there was a tap on the door and in came a jovial Ray to pass the time of day with my editor, Carl Moser. When he left, Carl explained to me who he was and that, although a New Bradwell man, he was very well known in Bletchley. A few months later I saw him again, but this time when I made my first visit to report on a Newport Pagnell RDC meeting, courtesy of a lift to Newport from my Aspley Guise home in the large Rover car of Woburn Sands hairdresser George Wesley, who

9

was also a member of the RDC. I recall, too, that while I was tucked up in luxury in the back seat, the front seat passenger was another councillor and Woburn Sands businessman representing the area, Mr Cyril Hutton.

Ernest Pye, who as I have mentioned earlier, was the Corporation's first chief engineer, was born in 1924. He and his wife now live in Passmore, Milton Keynes, and came to the area when Ernest joined the Corporation's staff in 1967. In local government all his life, Ernest grew up in St Helens, Lancashire, where his father worked at the famous Pilkington glass factory, as did almost every man in the town. Like Ray Bellchambers, Ernest also remembers how Bletchley councillors felt aggrieved in 1970 that, with the planners' concept of Milton Keynes given the green light following the inquiry into the interim report, its role as the civic and commercial centre of North Bucks was under threat.

He believes that the interpretation of the phrase 'multi-centred city' might well be the core of the problem, though at that time I know that the general feeling was that all the centres would be given equal prominence. However, Ernest thinks that as head of the MKDC Board, Lord Campbell always saw Central Milton Keynes as the new civic and commercial heart of the development, then as it expanded, of the district and of the region. Certainly by the time I joined the MKDC staff in 1989, Milton Keynes as a whole was being marketed vigorously as a regional centre, but I will come to that later.

There were certainly concerns at senior MKDC level, Ernest tells me, that Bletchley might get too strong in relation to other aspects of the overall Milton Keynes growth pattern. These concerns were probably brought about by Bletchley's positive approach to bringing more inward investment – and therefore more jobs – to the town and by its Council's recognition that the town's still growing population was crying out for better leisure facilities. Ironically, Milton Keynes was to face exactly the same demands, and combat them in very much the same way, a dozen or so years later.

The new Leisure Centre nears completion in the early 1970s. The Queen's Pool, with its covering, is in the foreground.

Bletchley's action at the time, however, was to open up the Mount Farm area to industry and commerce to support the successful Denbigh industrial estate, and the first factory unit to appear there was that of Compound Sections, which opened in the summer of 1970. Further units quickly followed.

On the leisure scene, the problem seemed initially to be handled with a 'cart-before-the-horse' basis, for to make way for a new, purpose-built Leisure Centre, which is still with us today, existing facilities had to go.

Though a Leisure Centre was something the town needed and was a feature the council was keen to provide, it was to be sited on what was then the open space known as Central Gardens. The gardens, sporting some beautiful beds of roses, were always very well maintained by the Council and provided a quiet haven to sit and watch the world go by. There was a putting green just inside the entrance to the right, now the carriageway of Princes Way, while there were hard tennis courts to the left, where a car park is today. As well as the Gardens themselves, the old Bletchley Printers offices and former Bletchley Gazette office were also demolished, as was the town's swimming pool,

A busy Queen's Pool before it was roofed over.

the Queen's Pool, to be replaced by what many in the town derisively called 'the duck pond' – a wide but shallow water feature that surrounded the new centre and which over the years was to become a dumping ground for all sorts of rubbish. The Queen's Pool, an open-air pool, had served the town well and was 'home' to Bletchley Swimming Club, formed in 1958. In its heyday the club had some 500 members and towards the end of its life it was roofed over while the finishing touches were made to the indoor pool inside the Leisure Centre.

At the far end of the town, in the wedge of land made by Buckingham Road and Tattenhoe Lane, leisure facilities were continued with the construction of the Windmill Hill golf course, so that by 1973 both leisure centre and golf course were up and running.

While the differences between MKDC and Bletchley simmered below the surface, the Development Corporation, in what it regarded as 'a goodwill gesture' to Bletchley, developed Stephenson House, an office block, and the Brunel Centre, a mix of retail outlets, on a site

The station end of Queensway before demolition made way for the Brunel Centre. Oliver Road is just beyond the Cowley and Wilson garage on the far left.

which ran at right angles to both sides of Queensway, taking in part of Albert Street and the former Park Street area on one side, and the old cattle market on the other.

At the southern end of this development – the cattle market area – supermarket giants Sainsbury's opened a store. Premises demolished to make way for the overall complex included the former North Bucks Times and Gazette offices at number five, Queensway, several retail premises and the fish and chip shop and cafe owned by a well-known Bletchley man, Norman Green. This development closed off direct traffic access from Queensway to Buckingham Road and the station, and its new culmination was given the name Stanier Square. In this former carriageway area, now bounded by the Co-op store, Boots the chemist and other shops to the western side, a large brick and concrete plinth was erected which was to have on it a full scale replica of a Stanier-type locomotive to commemorate Bletchley's railway heritage. But for

At a Liberal Association dance at Wilton Hall in the early 1970s are, left to right: Hazel and John Roberts, Don and Jan Waldron, Pat James, Bob Page, Bernard James, Barbara Page, Davinia Page, Les Page, Elaine Grayson.

reasons one supposes of finance, no loco ever appeared and the plinth was dismantled some years ago.

Ernest Pye recalls that the construction of the new road to give traffic its revised route to the station, and which was to pull Bletchley directly in to the new city's grid road system in the form of the dual-carriageway we now know as Saxon Street, was quite an engineering headache. Given the constraints caused by the railway line to one side and residential housing on the other, the new road took out the much used Albert Street playing field. On this site now is the Lidl supermarket, other retail outlets, a garage and car workshops, with its southern side being the spur road to Queensway, Prince's Way. Ernest was to stay with the Development Corporation until 1984, when he retired, serving for the last ten years as assistant general manager.

As the mid-1970s approached, Bletchley was positively booming and

Ladies of Bletchley WI and their guests at a 1970s party.

Queensway was a thriving shopping centre. Woolworths, Sketchley, Finlay, Halfords, Radio Rentals, Hatters the furnishers, Boots, W.H.Smith, Sainsbury's and many other national names traded alongside the local owner-occupier shops. These included Ted Neal's toy and pram shop, Bertie Irons' shoe shop, Weatherhead's radio and television sales premises and repair workshops and, beyond the Studio cinema, towards Fenny, Don Sewell's cycle shop and Gilroy's ladies fashions run by the Mason family. Sainsbury's, however, soon became the focal point of weekend grocery shopping for people from far afield, not least for those of us from the Bow Brickhill, Woburn Sands and Aspley Guise areas. I remember several Christmas shopping trips in the mid to late 1970s when the store was so busy that trolleys filled every aisle. It took ages to get through the shopping list and even longer to get to, and through, a checkout. If you didn't get into the adjacent car park before 8.30am on a Saturday morning, it was a job to find a parking space.

At the Queen's Silver Jubilee in 1977 these 'ladies' got together to play football at the St Thomas Aquinas school playing field in St Mary's Avenue. Among them are K.Pittock, K.Page, G.Wilby, E.Devoil, N.Devoil, D. Watts, J. Hibbert, S. Guthrie and D.Lennard.

The whole town had a vibrancy about it that was perhaps only matched by the immediate post-war years. Clubs and voluntary organisations prospered, the three major political parties – Conservative, Labour and Liberal – had positive footholds in the town and its outlying areas, unemployment was low and there was a general feeling of well-being.

While all this was taking place in Bletchley I was no longer close to the developmental action, as I had been earlier when plans for the new city were first formally announced in 1967. At that time I was the editor of The Bucks Standard in Newport Pagnell but in 1968 I left the newspaper and spent the next few months helping out at Bletchley Office Supplies, the business of the late Derek Blay with premises on the Watling Street, almost opposite the factory of Valentin, Ord and Nagle, at Fenny Stratford. The factory was demolished in 1983 and Wharfside now occupies the site. I then moved on to set up an office

16

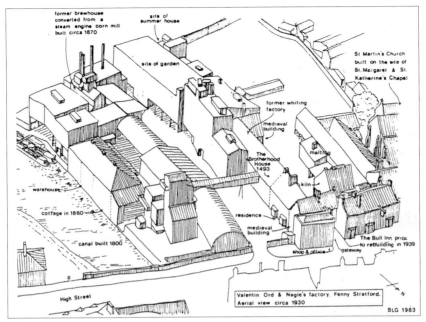

former brewhouse
converted from a
steam engine corn mill
built circa 1870

site of
summer house

St Martin's Church
built on the site of
St. Margaret & St.
Katherine's Chapel

site of garden

former whiting
factory

medieval
building

The
Brotherhood
House
1493

maltings

warehouse

kiln

cottage in 1880

residence

medieval
building

The Bull Inn prior
to rebuilding in 1939

canal built 1800

shop & office

gateway

High Street

Valentin Ord & Nagle's factory. Fenny Stratford.
Aerial view circa 1930

BLG 1983

A sketch of the Valentin, Ord and Nagle works in 1930. The factory was always known locally as 'Nagles' though around 1970 the premises were sold to Membray-Garton before being sold on again to the sugar refiners, Tate and Lyle. The factory was demolished in 1983.

in Queensway, on the site of what is now Ambassador House, for the Three Counties News Agency.

By September of 1969, however, I became one of the growing band of railway commuters from Bletchley to London where I joined the international publishers, Marshall Cavendish, as executive editor of a sports encyclopedia produced in weekly parts. Called 'The Game', it quickly established for itself a solid customer base.

It was a demanding job in those early days of my time with the company, for 'The Game' was running over budget and behind schedule and there were fears that we would not meet the launch date. But some procedural changes here and there, the recruitment of a new journalist to be my right-hand man and some long hours at the desk meant that we made it.

The picturesque fountain on Church Green, Bletchley, adjacent to Rectory Cottages, in 1972. The fountain was removed and the pool filled in soon after.

Floats in the Bletchley Carnival of 1975 parade along Queensway.

Bletchley's carnival queen of 1975, 21-years-old Eileen Carrington on the merry-go-round with her two attendants, Ann McNamara, 23, and Pat Grimmett, 17.

19

Milton Keynes mayor Pat Adams greets veterans at Bletchley's Remembrance Day in 1979.

When I joined the company there were one or two raised eyebrows that a 'country boy', as I know I was called, was in charge of a major launch and the implied question was there of could I really do it. But I must have got something right as within nine weeks of joining the company I was called to the office of the managing editor, a no-nonsense New Zealander named John Ruck, and told I was to be promoted.

As deputy managing editor the first thing I had to do, he said, was to bring more of the company's publications into line as I had done with the 'The Game'. So, it seemed, 'the country boy' had made good and I found myself responsible for all editorial aspects of half-a-dozen of the company's current publications, as well as becoming involved in the planning for newer titles. The money was good, I enjoyed the challenge and life looked to be on the up and up.

But all good things come to an end, so the saying goes, and after only two years with Marshall Cavendish a reconstruction of the company in what it called 'an uncertain economic climate' – some overseas sales were somewhat disappointing, I believe – meant several of us at senior

Young members of Bletchley brass band assemble for a pre-Christmas practice in 1979.

level were shown the door over a short period of time, albeit in the nicest possible way. John Ruck, I learned later, put his time to use when he left by opening up a games and model shop in Harrow.

For six months after I left Marshall Cavendish I worked once more on a local newspaper, the Beds and Bucks Observer at Leighton Buzzard, being deputy editor to Geoff South who, like me, had grown up in Aspley Guise but was then living in Ridgmont. His younger brother, John, also went into journalism after leaving school and carved himself out a rewarding career, I believe, in South Africa.

During this spell at Leighton I managed to get to grips with the game of golf, courtesy of the professional at Leighton's pleasant little course, but I was soon back to commuting to London when I joined the staff of the Inner London Education Authority (ILEA) late in 1971. So we were now well into the decade of the 1970s, a decade that began with The Sun introducing its avid male readers to Page 3 girls and Vivien Neves, a top model, shocking the establishment by appearing naked in an advertisement in The Times. Before us lay the three-day week under Ted

21

Heath's Conservative government as he fought the Unions and later, Labour premier Jim Callaghan posing the question: 'Crisis. What crisis?' when rubbish piled up in the streets and the cold months of 1978–79 became known as 'the winter of discontent'. That finished Jim Callaghan and in 1979 the country elected its first woman prime minister, Margaret Thatcher. On the social side, everyone wanted to dance to the long-playing record 'Saturday Night Fever' by the Bee-Gees as discotheques became all the rage.

Details of my time with ILEA beginning in 1971 can wait, but for now let me continue with what the late 1970s, and then the next twenty years, had in store for Bletchley.

CHAPTER 2

DECLINE AND FALL

The first public, but very positive, sign that Bletchley might in time lose its position as the major influence in North Bucks came at midnight on 31 March 1974, for it was then that Bletchley Urban Council ceased to exist and became amalgamated with Wolverton UDC, Newport Pagnell UDC and Newport RDC into a single new authority, Milton Keynes District Council.

Preparations for such a restructuring of North Bucks' local government had been ongoing for some time, of course, but when it actually occurred there were many in Bletchley and Fenny Stratford who wondered how the towns would fare with civic matters in the hands of non-Bletchley folk.

Initially, though, nothing seemed to change. Refuse collections carried on as normal, water still came out of the tap when you turned it on, the Bletchley District Gazette made its weekly appearance, Queensway was still a busy shopping thoroughfare and Bletchley and Fenny Stratford, increasingly referred to as a single entity, were literally bursting with activity. But radical change was to come, albeit still some years away.

Admittedly, Fenny Stratford had given over its position as the major shopping area to Queensway, but the decline in Fenny's fortunes had begun a little earlier in the post-war period following the Second World War victory in 1945. Throughout the 1950s, however, it was still a trading area to be reckoned with, and there were shops and offices doing steady business throughout the length and breadth of Aylesbury Street, as well as another parade of retail premises in Victoria Road and shops to be found in Simpson Road and fronting the Watling Street.

The A5 Watling Street, Aylesbury Street and Simpson Road crossroads at that time saw the heavy volume of traffic using the A5 Watling Street – the M1 was still almost ten years away – controlled by traffic lights. Mr Durrant's opticians' premises were prominent on the Watling Street–Aylesbury Street corner opposite St Martin's church, hence it still being referred to currently by many as Durrant's corner. Running along Aylesbury Street on that side of the road then were Cook's, the greengrocer's, Alfie Duffield's shop which sold the best working wear such as overalls and boiler suits that a man could find anywhere, Axford's the newsagents, Charles Mare's the gents outfittters, a butcher's shop, Healey's cafe, Pacey's – now Pollard's – the ironmongers, Mr Salmon's teashop and grocers, Mr Vigor's chemists, Phyllis Cooper's hairdressing, where my wife, Barbara, was apprenticed, and Cowlishaw's the drapers, to name but some. The other side of Aylesbury Street housed the fish and chip shop – as it still does – Fortescue's garage, Papworth's grocers, Godden's the fruiterers and florists, Ray Lubbock's photographic studio and offices, and others.

These included perhaps Fenny's best known trader, Mr Golding, who ran an ice cream shop. Mr Golding's ice cream constantly won awards at trade shows throughout the country and I know he was approached many times by the major national ice cream makers and distributors to sell them his recipe. But to the best of my knowledge he turned down the offers and the secret of his wonderful ice cream went with him to the grave.

Opposite Durrant's corner, near to The Swan on the Watling Street, were the premises of J.D.Bushell, the wholesale and retail grocers, Blackmore's, who made and distributed the paper patterns used by ladies making their own dresses, Vaughan's newsagents and Janet Hill's greengrocery store. The Bridge pub completed this run of shops, with the Kings Head pub – now Pink Punters – a little further on towards Bow Brickhill. All in all, Fenny was still very much alive in the 1950s, but twenty years later, with Queensway's residential buildings having

Fenny Stratford in the days when it still held sway over Bletchley. The canal fronting the gas works can be clearly seen centre-top, with the A5 Watling Street running at an angle across the picture from left to right. The County cinema is the large building bottom left with Woodbine Terrace in the very bottom left corner. Church Street, with its two pedestrians and two vehicles, is centre, bottom to top. The curve of the Bletchley–Bedford railway line can just be seen, top left.

become shops and offices, Fenny was in serious decline. One by one the family businesses went and the shops seemed to change hands and become something different on an all too regular basis. The overall pace of life seemed to be quickening day by day, but for Fenny, its commercial life began to slow and gradually ebb away.

Eileen Corden remembers both the busy times and Fenny falling away to take second place behind Bletchley as the main shopping area, for her husband, Peter, and her father-in-law, 'Jimmy' Corden, were both chemists who ran a successful business from premises in Victoria Road.

'Jimmy' Corden began the venture in 1922 and said little when the eldest of his four sons decided on a career as an engineer. But the other three, of whom Peter was one, were told categorically that they were to follow in father's footsteps and become chemists. This they duly did and Peter began working in the Victoria Road shop when he was 21, in 1944. He was called up into the army shortly afterwards and had only just finished his basic training when the Second World War came to an end. By this time, however, he and Eileen Haddon, who lived with her family at 31 Brooklands Road, Bletchley, decided to get married and on New Year's Day, 1946, a family conference decided that, with clothes rationing still in force, they would pool their clothing coupons for the two young people to use when buying their wedding outfits.

Eileen recalls that they did their shopping in Northampton, with Peter intent on buying some good civilian-style shoes – Northampton was then the centre of the footwear industry – as, still in the army, he did not want to marry in uniform. Eileen bought herself a nice light blue two-piece suit and they were married by the Rev. Cyril Wheeler at St Martin's, Fenny Stratford, on 7 January, 1946, with a reception where their wedding cake was made by the Co-op. The rest of the food they provided themselves.

Two years later, in 1948, Peter left the army – he served with the Ox and Bucks regiment – and was back behind the counter in Victoria Road. That same year the National Health Service was born and, in common with the rest of the Fenny traders, the shop was very busy.

By the late 1970s, as I have already mentioned, Fenny was feeling the pinch and playing second fiddle to Queensway. And by the 1980s, as Queensway itself began to decline following the opening of the Lloyds Court and main shopping complexes in Central Milton Keynes, the decline almost became a free-fall. Of the main Fenny shops Pollard's were still trading in Aylesbury Street – as they still are – but many other buildings had gone, including the Spurgeon Memorial Baptist chapel on the south side and now home to a car showroom. In Victoria Road Peter Corden called it a day in 1988, selling the shop on to continue as a chemist, but that has now gone and the premises trade as a tattooist.

Corden's chemist shop in the 1970s is flanked by the Milton Keynes DIY Centre and a range of other retail outlets.

A 'This Is Your Life' party for Canon Wright who retired as vicar of St Martin's, Fenny Stratford, at Christmas, 1979, aged 66. Milton Keynes mayor Pat Adams was a special guest at the party.

Colgrove's, the butchers, were among the last of the 'old' names to go, closing their Victoria Road shop towards the end of the 1990s. The Co-op store on the corner of Denmark Street has also gone and is now occupied by Londis.

For Peter Corden, retirement meant more time to enjoy his game of bowls with St Martin's bowls club – his father 'Jimmy' bowled for Bletchley Town bowls club – and I played many a pleasant game with him some years ago. Sadly, Peter died in 1995, though Eileen continues to live in the same Eaton Avenue house that they shared throughout their married life. A keen photographer, Eileen has a wonderful collection of photographs of Bletchley landmarks throughout the years.

Many Fenny Stratford shopkeepers – Peter Corden among them – and businesses were members of the Bletchley Chamber of Trade in those early post-war days and right up to the late 1970s. The Chamber of Trade, alongside many other of the twin-town organisations, did much for charity, and its annual ball at Wilton Hall was one of the social highlights of the year. In 1974, however, the first signs of wear in Bletchley's fabric were only just around the corner and began to appear positively by the end of the decade. By this time the managers of the newer, corporate shops, which gradually replaced the former owner-occupied commercial premises throughout Bletchley and Fenny, began to turn their backs on the organisation.

Like other groups in the town, such as the Rotary Club, the Lions, the various churches, Women's Institutes, sports clubs and youth organisations in those post-war years, the Chamber believed the town of Bletchley was something that mattered and was something of which to be proud.

Nothing shouted Bletchley's pride more loudly than the 1974 Town Pageant, written by Douglas Loak, who was a stalwart of the town's Bletchco Players drama group and a most able writer and director.

Written and performed to mark the winding up of Bletchley Council, the pageant traced Bletchley's heritage from pre-Roman times through to the then present day – 1974 – and was a first-rate and unique production of which Douglas is still justly proud. It was performed at the new Leisure Centre for a week, with one of its most moving scenes being that in which, on its final night, the four chairmen of the various councils which were to disappear took off their chains of office to herald the arrival of Milton Keynes' first mayor, Councillor Ernest Fryer.

President of the Bletchley Chamber of Trade at this time was Bert Irons who, with his wife, Maisie, ran a very successful shoe shop in Queensway. They were very well known in North Bucks and played a prominent part in many aspects of Bletchley life. At the time, I recall, their shop was the only one in Bletchley which stocked Clarks shoes, and in those days to have – and so to be able to afford – Clarks shoes was very much a feather in your cap.

Under Bert Irons' stewardship the Chamber held its own until the late 1970s and then, as I have mentioned, membership began to tail off. The managers of the newer corporate and chain-store shops were very often people who lived far from Bletchley. Understandably, perhaps, their main priority was to turn in good trading results and being part of the community was not that high on the agenda. When it came to six o'clock their thoughts were focused on how quickly could they get to Bicester, Northampton, Luton or wherever was their home so that they could spend time with their families. Not for them a relaxing half-hour or so in the company of other town traders discussing local problems over a glass of something before going home for dinner. So, with the coming of the multi-outlet premises, shopping in Bletchley began to lose its personal touch.

Born in Lancashire in 1942, a young Stanley Green came to Aspley Guise four years later to live with his parents at number 24 Spinney Lane, the end house in a small run of properties facing an open field and Aspley's Bedford Road to the front. As he came to the end of his schooldays at Aspley Heath school, Stan did some odd-job gardening for an Amercian, a Mr Oakley, who lived in a larger house further along the lane and who worked at the U.S base at Chicksands. Stan remembers enjoying the odd run in Mr Oakley's big American car, one day being taken all the way to Stratford-on-Avon, a substantial journey for a youngster who spent virtually all of his time in Aspley Guise!

When he left school at 15 Stan became a fireman on the railway, based at Bletchley, for five years, before spending the next five years with another organisation synonomous with Bletchley, Terrapin. This led him on to lorry driving for Marston Valley brickworks at Brogborough before he set up in business with his own lorry.

In 1965 Stan married Pam Denton, who lived at New Bradwell. Pam was born above the fish and chip shop run by her grandmother at Corner Pin in the village, and the newly-weds set up home in King Edward Street, not far from Corner Pin. When Pam's grandma decided to retire in 1970, she did a house-swop with Stan and Pam who took over running the shop. It was to be the start of many years in the catering trade, for two years later they took premises at Ryde in the Isle of Wight before returning in 1974 to take over a cafe and fish and chip shop in Bletchley.

Bletchley's shopping thoroughfare in its days as Bletchley Road, and then later as Queensway, had both a cafe and 'chippie' in one building, the premises run by a well-known Bletchley man, Norman Green. Norman's cafe and 'chippie' was swept away in the development of the Brunel Centre in the early 1970s, but new premises were found for the business at the eastern end of the new complex, Weatherburn Court, with Stephenson House as its neighbour. Though Norman Green no longer ran the business, it being leased to a man named Harold Faithful at the time, another Green – Stan – took over in 1974. Appropriately, it seemed to Stan, the business had traded under the name of Greenways, which suited him perfectly and he found as his new neighbours Barclay's Bank, an estate agency run by the Blue Boar group, the Co-op cleaners and a William Hill betting shop.

Quickly settling in at the Weatherburn Court premises, Stan joined the Bletchley Chamber of Trade and was given a warm welcome by Bert Irons and other members. He soon became involved in the Chamber's

Weatherburn Court before its demolition in 1999.

activities, working to keep up membership, and by the end of the decade was the Chamber's chairman. In 1981 he succeeded Bert Irons as president.

At that time, Stan tells me, the membership of the Chamber was already down to twenty, and, try as he might, ably assisted by vice-chairman John Mather, who ran the Topburger premises in Queensway, no headway was made. The Chamber kept up its work in providing Queensway with Christmas lights until the mid-80s but by then, Stan recalls, very few traders wanted to be

Stan Green wearing his badge of office as President of the Bletchley Chamber of Trade.

31

involved in contributing to the cost so the initiative floundered. Not until some years later did Queensway see Christmas lights return, and that was when the Council stepped in to resurrect the idea.

In 1999 and after only 25 years of life, Weatherburn Court was demolished for redevelopment and Stan Green's business relocated to the opposite end of the Brunel Centre, next door to Sainsbury's, where he continues to trade today. As I write, new premises scheduled to be taken by Wilkinsons' department store, with a health club above, are being erected on the old Weatherburn Court/Barclays Bank site. Technically, the Bletchley Chamber of Trade still exists, for it has never been formally wound up. Stan is still therefore its president, and retains his badge of office, Bruce Pollard, who has the Fenny Stratford irongmonger's business, is treasurer, and there is still a bank account with money in it. What it doesn't have is members.

As the family-run shops throughout the Bletchley–Woburn Sands–Aspley Guise corridor began to fall at the expense of a growing Milton Keynes, so the older industries suffered too. The brickworks at Brogborough closed in the early 1980s with Bletchley's Jubilee Works at Skew Bridge on the Drayton Parslow Road going almost ten years before that. Originally a Flettons operation, but then taken over by the London Brick Company, this works had its early electricity supply provided by a submarine engine. Later, it was hooked into the mains supply. Bletchley's major brick making plant, the yard at Newton Longville, closed down in the mid-80s as the demand for bricks tailed right off when house building techniques employed more timber framing and concrete blocks for internal walls.

Jack Bromfield, who lives in Newton Road, Bletchley and who was made redundant when the Newton Longville plant closed, makes an interesting point, though, about the workforce of the brick industry during the immediate post war period and right up to the 1980s. In these days of racial awareness, comments Jack, you had in the brickworks during that period English, Irish, Scots and Welsh, Poles, Lithuanians, Hungarians and Italians, Pakistanis, Indians and other Asians

The boarded-up Rodex factory on the Watling Street just before it came down and the site used to build the Tesco supermarket.

all working harmoniously together. In Jack's view it begs the question of what's gone wrong and what part, if any, has the growing race relations industry itself played in the heightening of tensions?

In Bletchley the brush factories were long gone, Tetley's vacated their premises in Osborne Street which is currently under development for a sheltered housing scheme, and W. O. Peake's operation at the Rodex factory on the Watling Street, where high class clothing was made under the Aquascutum brand for many years, is now home to Tesco's.

Betty Young grew up in Denmark Street, Bletchley, and after leaving school joined Peake's at the age of 14 in 1942. She was pleased to have got the job; in those days the Bletchley view was that women's work was either the brush factories or Peake's, with the 'better class' girls going to Peake's.

Starting as a trainee hand-sewer on the ladies clothing side, Betty moved on through the sewing operations into the cutting rooms where she worked on ladies suits and skirts. She quite literally had a hand in making garments for our own royal family, for foreign heads of state and

Manager George White, who lived in Manor Road, Bletchley, watches machinists at the Rodex factory in the 1950s.

other VIPs from all over the world, and for Margaret Thatcher during her years as the British premier. Most of the styles for the royal household and others had names, she recalls, but for Mrs Thatcher it was more down to earth – style one, style two, style three, for example. Airlines also had Rodex making their air hostess uniforms and Betty remembers that each uniform had to have two skirts to one top. And all tailored to a diminutive size eight! Special airline-logo buttons were sent to be stitched on to the uniforms but many went missing, Betty says, because they made wonderful souvenirs!

In 1958 Betty married a Bletchley railwayman, Eddie Abbot, who she recalls was thrilled to bits when he qualified as a train driver. The couple lived in Western Road, Bletchley, before moving to Bow Brickhill in 1964. With Eddie suffering poor health, they moved back to Bletchley in 1976 but Eddie died in 1980.

After 48 years with Peake's as a family company, Betty left in 1990 when it was sold to a Japanese organisation. The Watling Street factory was vacated and new premises were opened at Tilbrook. Betty remembers how working patterns at Rodex changed throughout the

Cutting the 21st anniversary cake of the Rodex Social Club in the 1950s. Mr Blyth, the general manager, does the honours alongside Miss Washington, a relative of the Peake family who owned the works.

Girls from the Rodex factory at its Social Club's 21st birthday party in the mid-1950s.

Betty Abbott and her husband, Eddie, pictured in the garden of their Western Road home in the early 1960s.

1970s, particularly when a bonus system was brought in, and many folk would have then turned their back on work when she left there at the age of 62. But she used the lady's prerogative of taking a couple of years off her total when she applied for a domestic job at Milton Keynes General hospital in 1991. She got the job and thoroughly enjoyed her years there, finally taking retirement in 2001.

As Bletchley and Fenny Stratford became more and more urbanised through-out the 1970s, one side of life began to give particular cause for concern – the policing of the joint communities and of the neighbouring villages.

At that time most villages had a police house which was home to the local sergeant or constable and as such a uniformed officer was a common enough site at any time of the day or night. For those villages without such provision, the nearest based officer would often appear. Living in Bow Brickhill, as I did then, this meant we saw Roy Kimber from Woburn Sands patrolling on his motorbike and when Roy moved on, Rodney Abbot took over.

In Bletchley and Fenny, however, physical changes were perhaps more noticeable, for the old police station in Simpson Road, Fenny Stratford, was taken out of operation in 1969 and by the early 1970s a new police

The former Bletchley and Fenny Stratford police station in Simpson Road, closed in 1969.

station had opened on the corner of Sherwood Drive and Buckingham Road, close to Bletchley railway station and adjacent to the new Fire Station, built in 1972.

It was to these new premises that Tim Hill, a superintendent serving at Cowley, Oxford came in 1977 as deputy to the then chief superintendent and divisional commander, Stan Crump. The old Buckinghamshire Constabulary had disappeared in 1968 and in its place came the force we have today, Thames Valley, made up of the amalgamation of five separate authorities – Bucks, Berks, Oxfordshire, Oxford City and Reading Borough.

Tim remembers that the

Chief Superintendent Tim Hill.

37

problem uppermost at the time was the lack of police presence in the public's eye as, indeed, it still is today. Though there was a determination to keep village-based officers wherever possible, a lack of manpower meant that one officer needed to then police a much larger area. One way this was being tackled was by the use of the Panda car, which had been introduced in the late 1960s.

It was argued that the car could transport an officer over a wide area quickly and efficiently and its presence would be a deterrent to would-be criminals. Money was forthcoming from the Home Office to supply forces throughout the country with Pandas and they soon became recognised by the public. But what the sight of a distinctive small car could not do, of course, was to have the individual character and physical identity of a person, which is what the public wanted and is now recognised by police authorities generally.

By April 1980 Stan Crump had moved on to become deputy chief constable in Cambridge and Tim was promoted to chief superintendent and divisional commander. By now Milton Keynes was growing rapidly and he was faced with the same old problem. How to police an expanding area with manpower that was not increasing. He remembers lunching with Her Majesty's Inspector of Constabulary at the MKDC headquarters at Wavendon Tower in 1981 and pulling out all the stops he knew to get more officers allocated to him.

The result was, his division was given all five officers that the Inspector was prepared to give to the whole of the Thames Valley force that year, so Tim was not the most popular man with his fellow senior officers from the other constituent areas. But even five additional men for a place growing bigger and bigger day by day was really laughable.

One of Bletchley's problem areas at the time was the Lakes Estate and Tim decided to 'patch police' the area. This meant allocating a sergeant, four men and a woman officer to the estate with the brief to get themselves known, respected and above all, trusted. Within a year, when crime in the division overall had risen by thirteen per cent, crime on the Lakes Estate had not gone up at all. So well had the personnel

At the Bletchley Police Ball held at Wilton Hall on 10 November 1978, Milton Keynes mayor Bert Eley, right, with guests.

on the ground done their job that if an officer who was not part of the six strong team went on to the estate, his appearance was almost resented and it was made clear he was not welcomed!

As the 1980s progressed, policies such as this had to change because of financial pressures and it was clear, at the same time, that the Panda had had its day. Police authorities throughout the country recognised there was no substitute for the 'bobby-on-the-beat' approach but, as ever, it boiled down to money and manpower.

Alongside what I will call the sharp end of the job, Tim was heavily involved at this time in the planning of the new divisional police headquarters to be built in Central Milton Keynes. His administration moved into the new building in June 1985 and one of his major responsibilities was to decide how now to police the ever expanding area as an urban city, rather than as a collection of rural communities, and at the same time to allocate his slender manpower resources in such a way as to maintain a community spirit.

Working closely with the director of social development, Peter

Open day at the Central Milton Keynes police station on Sunday 8 September 1985. Pictured are Darryl Elmore and Gary Eccles, of Furzton, astride the motor-cycle of PC Roderick Hardie.

Waterman, Tim's thinking was to allocate a 'village' constable to each area of the city now growing out of the original villages. He believed that this approach would achieve more of a community feel to the policing system rather more than the detached urban style. Initially, he says, it was considered a waste of manpower but as development within the grid square was completed, it was community policing in its real sense.

During his years in charge at Milton Keynes Tim Hill worked hard at getting himself known so that any moans and groans about the police were directed at the organisation he headed rather than at individual officers. He retired in March 1987 but was still in the public eye when he became the founder-chief executive of the Milton Keynes Community Trust, now renamed Foundation, one of eight experimental trusts in the country aimed at setting up endowment funds which would provide a permanent source of funding for the voluntary sector.

Retiring from the Trust a little over two years ago, Tim is now chairman of the Milton Keynes Living Archive and a patron of the

Macmillan Cancer Relief Milton Keynes Appeal. He is a member of the Rotary Club of Bletchley, which was formed in 1957, and has twice held office as its president. Tim lives with his wife, Theresea, on Windmill Hill, Bletchley and still firmly believes that if officers can be seen on the streets, then the public perception is that the forces of law and order are at work.

When Tim Hill called it a day at Central Milton Keynes police station in 1987, Queensway was but a pale image of what it was 15 years earlier. With the main shopping complex in Central Milton Keynes opening in the early 1980s, and the Centre coming later in 1988, the lengthening shadows of Milton Keynes were fast bringing a twilight to Bletchley which it had never imagined. During the 1990s the situation worsened. Major players in the shopping league opened on Bletchley's own Watling Street and the town found itself entering a completely new social era.

CHAPTER 3

BUSY BRICKHILL

Douglas Loak and his wife Christine viewed 1970 with some trepidation, for the boundary of the new city of Milton Keynes came literally to within a few yards of their home and garden at Bow Brickhill. Indeed, the only thing between them and what they knew would one day be an industrial area was the village railway crossing on the Bletchley–Bedford line.

Their home, Four Winds, into which they moved in 1954 after they were married, is a pleasant house on the junction of the main Woburn Sands–Bow Brickhill–Bletchley road and what is now Brickhill Street. In 1970 this modern city road was still a quiet little lane leading to the hamlet of Caldecote. Christine is the daughter of former Bow Brickhill publican Eustace Stone and his wife, Mary, so is a village girl through and through; Douglas worked for nearly 40 years at Hanslope Park before retiring in 1987. Their Brickhill neighbours in 1970 were on one side the crossing keeper, John Pugh, who lived with his family in the railway house alongside the hand-operated crossing gates, and on the other side Percy Collins, a real Bow Brickhill character who was postman, taxi-driver and paraffin seller to the village. Percy's old bungalow has gone now, replaced some years ago by the substantial dwelling of local businessman, Roy Toombs, and the railway house was demolished in the 1980s.

Early in 1970 the Loaks had a taste of what was to come when the firm of Reed's opened their plant manufacturing aluminium cans just the other side of the railway crossing. Luckily this was not part of the long

42

term plan for the site, but even so the noise and vibration experienced then by the Loaks was horrendous. At one stage they thought the village was being hit by an earthquake when ornaments fell off shelves, lamps shook, and a lavatory was broken. They quickly realised it was no earthquake but vibrations from the adjacent factory, complained immediately and the works duty officer, to his credit, came to see them straight away.

He agreed the nuisance was bad, so some of the equipment was resited, but the problem never really went away until the site was later redeveloped into what we know today. In the interim, windows in the house continued to rattle at certain times and things were no better when Reed's moved to make way for a similar manufacturing company, American Can. MKDC's Lord Campbell opened this new factory and commemorated the opening by planting a poplar tree. It promptly died.

In the 1980s the corner outside Four Winds was turned from a T-junction into the alignment there today and in the process the pavement outside the Loaks' front gate somehow disappeared. It has never been put back, but pavement or not, the new layout did not stop a succession of accidents occurring at the corner as traffic flows increased and drivers misjudged the severity of the turns.

It was around this time, too, that a little further along the lane the fine old thatched farmhouse known as Caldecote Farm was demolished to make way for the initial development of the Tilbrook area. For this development the American Can area was also cleared, so giving the Loaks final respite from the factory vibrations. But other problems were to come. Around 1990 Douglas and Christine awoke one morning to find a band of travellers making their home in the paddock field nearest Bletchley and immediately opposite their home, a field used years before by Christine's father, uncle Syd, and cousin Colin as a smallholding. This particular band of travellers didn't give them any trouble, were polite and often came to the house to use the 'phone; but when they moved on their replacement travellers were totally different.

In June of 1993 Douglas had to call the Milton Keynes Council's

A scene from 'Captain Carvallo' performed in 1980 by the Bletchco Players. Left to right are: Jim Clent, Alan Thompson, Adrian Schofield, Terry Roberts and Christine Loak.

travellers' liaison officer because of all the noise being made. It seemed that some of the group had returned at four o'clock in the morning from a holiday in Spain and by way of celebration, lit a huge bonfire around which they danced, singing and shouting at the tops of their voices. Daylight revealed broken glass all over the paddock.

Life in Four Winds, however, does have its better memories and not least of these are Douglas and Christine's recollections of the arts in Milton Keynes. As I have written earlier, it was Douglas who scripted the Bletchley Pageant in 1974, and even earlier than this both he and Christine were stalwarts of the Bletchco Players, an amateur dramatic group formed in Bletchley in 1944 to celebrate the centenary of the town's Co-operative society. A pageant celebrated this event, too, and well-known Bletchley men such as Bill Shaw and Tom Cloran, among others, formed Bletchco who performed three productions a year for many years. Douglas joined in 1949 and in 1957 Bletchco were the first winners of the highly prestigious Sir Laurence Olivier annual award for

The Ascot chorus from 'My Fair Lady' performed by the Milton Keynes Operatic Society in May 1984.

amateur dramatic societies. In its earlier days Bletchco met at the Co-op hall in Albert Street before moving on to a hall, complete with stage, in Warwick Road. But then the local authority needed the space, there was no new home, and, after almost fifty years, Bletchco Players were no more.

Alongside Bletchco Players Douglas also has an interest in Bletchley Operatic Society, which was formed in 1953 following a meeting called by former Bletchley Gazette proprietor, Ron Staniford. The Society performed its first work in 1954, changed its name to the Milton Keynes Operatic Society in the 1970s and, from 1988–1997, Douglas Loak was its chairman. But it is for his work over nearly thirty years with John Dankworth's Wavendon All Music Plan that Douglas, with Christine by his side, is perhaps best remembered. During this time Douglas was called upon to undertake many different tasks for the organization, but mostly his role was that of senior house manager. In this capacity he has many memories of the celebrities he escorted on their visits to

Douglas Loak greets Princess Margaret on one of her regular visits to the Wavendon All Music Plan.

Wavendon, either as performers or guests, and cherishes among them those of the late Princess Margaret, who was a great fan of the Wavendon concept.

Another man concerned in 1970 with the proximity of Milton Keynes on his doorstep was Don Burgess, a young farmer living with his wife, Eileen, and three sons, Alan, Andrew and Peter, at Tilbrook Farm, which fronted Station Road. There were four working farms in the village itself at that time – six if you counted Crossroads Farm close to the Watling Street and run for many years by the Gurney family, and Freda Unwin's Dropshort Farm, many years ago once a pub, on the Watling Street itself. Both the latter fall within Brickhill's parish boundary. Don farmed some fifty acres spread along the Woburn Sands–Bow Brickhill road and over the railway crossing where the Development Corporation wanted fifteen acres. Don, Eileen and the boys were very much part of the community and Don had played for the village football team in the 1960s, allowing us to use a field along the Woburn Sands road as a pitch.

But the MKDC ultimatum effectively took away a large chunk of his livelihood and there was no option other than to make a fresh start

Two of the classes at Bow Brickhill school in the early 1970s with teachers Mrs Hewitson, above, and Mrs Horsall, below.

elsewhere. By the autumn of 1971 the Burgess family had left Bow Brickhill to farm on the borders of Northants and Oxfordshire and Don, now retired, and Eileen still live in that area now. Over the next few years all the village farms disappeared – Barry Haynes left Rectory Farm which was taken over by Joe Carter, who to do so left Manor Farm which became the private house home of Donald and Diana Apps – Diana ran the village Brownie pack; John Colgrove left Poplars' Farm; and in the fullness of time Joe Carter called it a day at Rectory Farm. Crossroads Farm also went into non-farming hands, as I believe did Dropshort. What was a staple part of Bow Brickhill's heritage and commercial viability disappeared as Milton Keynes mushroomed.

After the runaway success of the Bow Brickhill football team in the early 1960s, to which I referred in my earlier book 'Changing Faces, Changing Places', the village football club then ran a reserve side as well to ensure that village boys were given a game. But with the first team still dominated by lads from outside, who began to drift away when the results went against them, coupled with the village interest overall gradually dropping off, by the mid-1960s the football club had closed down.

But football was not the be all and end all of community life in the village and by 1970 Bow Brickhill seemed to have captured some of the vibrancy associated with nearby Bletchley. Under the headship of Geoff Tremayne the school was a focal point of interest, with a thriving parent-teacher organisation and a pre-school playgroup; All Saints church, with Ronnie Groves-Brookes as rector, was well supported at its family services, and at its Harvest Festival it was, literally, standing room only; the Women's Institute branch and the two main political parties, Conservative and Labour, were also active. The village then still had a corner shop run by Mrs Holmes, while Mrs Lizzie West ran the Post Office from her home in Station Road – taken over by Mrs Holmes at the shop when Mrs West later retired – and The Wheatsheaf pub did a steady trade.

All in all, it was a very busy but pleasant village retreat, but it did lack

Children in costume for the Nativity play at Bow Brickhill school in December, 1971.

sporting activity. That changed in 1970, however, with the formation of the Bow Brickhill Sports and Social Club, brought about initially by two village teenage brothers, Anton and Gerald Crosby, the sons of Ron and Pat Crosby, approaching me with a request to reform the football club. A quick word on my part with former team manager Ken Burton, and the rector, as former president, resulted in a public meeting being held in the Church Hall which attracted a very large crowd. Although initially the agenda was merely to restart the football club, it was clear the village wanted more and by the end of the evening we had agreed to try and cater for the sporting needs of most of the community. It was a tall order.

Asked to be chairman of the new organisation I was ably assisted by the rector, Ken Burton, Gordon Heap, Peter Holland, Geoff Tremayne and many others to formulate a policy that addressed the inaugural meeting's wishes. What transpired, and very quickly too, was an organisation that operated like a small consortium of businesses, each section of 'business' catering for a particular sport or interest. So we had football, cricket, tennis, badminton, angling and youth-club sections, who ran their own affairs but reported back to an executive committee. This executive was made up of the senior officers – chairman, secretary and treasurer – supported by representatives from the various sections.

Monies were raised collectively by the executive via social functions such as dances, jumble sales, coffee mornings and the like, and each section was given a working float from these central monies. If a section made additional monies over and above its working float, then these monies went back into the central pool. The only sections actually operating in the village, though, were the football and youth sections, for tennis and badminton were played at Bletchley, the fishermen fished wherever they could, and the occasional game of cricket was always played away as there was no proper ground. That problem was to be resolved later with the coming of the village sports field; meantime, a canvas of the whole village resulted in almost eighty per cent of the teenage and adult population joining the new organisation.

The footballers played initially in the field immediately next door to Don Burgess's Tilbrook Farm – courtesy of Don yet again, though not the best of playing surfaces – but it was a start. Paul West, now a successful builder in Milton Keynes but still living in Bow Brickhill, will remember that pitch well. He broke his leg on it in that first season and, to the best of my knowledge, never played again. By August the next year, 1971, the side was playing on a field just the other side of the railway crossing, one of the fields that MKDC was to take from Don and now home to a roundabout and part of Brickhill Street.

Just inside the gateway to the field was a large ash tree from which, that year, I cut myself a reasonable walking stick. I still have the stick today, the tree is still there but now has the road on its 'wrong side', and I have fond memories of that field as both an excellent source of meat for the pot, for I shot many a hare there, and, of course, for its footballing connotations.

At a Bow Brickhill Sports and Social Club dance in the early 1970s are, left to right: Don Barden, John Pugh, Jean Pugh, Jess Odell, Bill Rawlings, Vera Rawlings, Fred West, Mary West, Alroy Pickersgill, Ann Pickersgill, Betty Barden.

Three years before the Sports and Social Club was formed, my wife Barbara and I, with our two children, Mark, who was then seven, and Rachel, 15 months, moved from The Pines in Church Road, Bow Brickhill to the small new development of Edwin Close, just across the road. We had lived in the village since we were married in 1957, Barbara being the daughter of George and Ivy Whittaker who lived in London Lane. At about the same time, Alroy Pickersgill, a Ridgmont lad by then running his own business as a painting and decorating contractor, moved into the house next door to Mrs Holmes' shop on the corner of Church Road. Alroy was married – and still is, I hasten to add – to Ann Payne, of Woburn Sands, the daughter of Stan Payne who lived in Woburn for many years, while the couple's two young children, Mark and Diane, completed the family.

Alroy was very well-known on the local sports scene, playing football for Winslow at the time, I believe, and being no mean cricketer either.

But with the emergence of the Sports and Social Club he was soon wearing a Brickhill shirt and with his experience of a higher class of football, Ken Burton quite rightly made him captain. By 1972 Alroy's experience and sheer presence on the field took Bow Brickhill to the final of the Division 3 knock-out competition of the North Bucks league, so emulating the success of the 1960s side. For me, lightning struck twice, for I was a reserve for the '60s game and my name could be found in the same position on the team sheet for the '72 final! Whatever, the game was played at Wicken, and we beat Plessey 3–2 in extra time, Pete Holland scoring the winner with a near post back-header in the gathering gloom. Only eleven medals were struck for the game, though participating clubs could request additional medals later, so it was typical of Alroy that before he went up to receive the trophy, he took me to one side and said: 'When I get my medal, I'll hand it back so you can collect it as yours at the end of the line.' It was a sporting gesture I will never forget and yes, Ken Burton saw to it that an extra medal was purchased for me a little later.

I didn't know it at the time, of course, but I wasn't to see out another full season as a player. The next year, at the age of 39, I took a whack under the left eye in a clash of heads in a league game and Ken Burton thought enough was enough for an old fellow like me! I had a lovely black eye the next morning, Sunday, and felt like I had the grandfather of all hangovers. I washed and shaved gingerly, then cleaned my teeth. And that's when I found out what the real damage was.

The bang under the left eye had jarred down through my jaw to one of my lower teeth which had split horizontally. It was a bit of a mess, so I put a 'phone call through to my dentist, Ken Adam, who had not long taken over from Laurie Costigan at the dental surgery then on Aspley Heath. Ken Lived in Mount Pleasant, Aspley Guise, and asked if I felt well enough to drive to his home for an initial examination. I drove to Aspley, from there we went to the surgery on Aspley Heath, and, at the end of an hour or so, Ken had repaired the damage to the tooth, or at least, what was left of it.

He did an excellent job; it's still going strong and when I go to him now at his Theydon Avenue, Woburn Sands, premises for my regular check-up, we often reminisce about that Sunday in 1973 and what we call my football tooth. It wasn't quite the end of my playing days though, for I turned out for 'quiet' pre-season friendlies and played in charity games, the last one at the age of 50 on Boxing Day, 1984.

Now, according to Bow Brickhill parish records, the need for a village playing field was first recognised in the late 1800s and often raised at Parish Council meetings over the ensuing years. But finally, in 1972, a public meeting was called to discuss purchasing eight acres of land at Poplars' Farm, the proposal being that a limited number of houses be built on a new road which would give access to a proposed sports field. The cost to the village, the meeting was told, would be £5000, half of which would be borrowed by the Parish Council from the Public Works Loan Board. The meeting voted 37 in favour of the proposal, no-one voted against, but there were five abstentions. To steer the project through, and to act as an intermediary between the Parish Council and the Sports and Social Club, who would be its main users, the Bow Brickhill Playing Field Committee was established.

While the village patted itself on the back with regard the breakthough, large chunks of the woodland at the top of Bow Brickhill's steep hill were being ravaged to cater for top class golfers. The first of the golf courses which now make up the greens, bunkers and fairways of the Woburn Golf and Country Club were under construction and the Parish Council called yet another public meeting to discuss the issue. As at Woburn Sands in relation to the mining of Fullers Earth, which I examine in the next chapter, there were many in Bow Brickhill who resented what they saw as an attack on the environment by Bedford Estates, the owners of the land in question. This resentment certainly surfaced at 'the golf course meeting' as it was always later remembered, particularly when one gentleman representing the golfing administrators tried to tell villagers that the project 'was not there to make money'. He was laughed out of the hall! Certainly over the next

The playing field pavilion, obtained from Maulden Bowls Club, with its additional units.

few years those woodland areas looked a mess until the new course settled down, and many favourite walks for villagers became no-go areas. But I confess now, some 30 years on, all the courses constructed look an absolute picture and the area as a whole is still pleasant walking – and horse riding – country.

Meanwhile, work on the levelling of the new playing field went on, though drainage was a problem, but on 2 March 1975 the field was opened, accessed by a road given the name Rushmere Close. Personally, I've often wondered why it wasn't called 'Colgrove Close' as a mark of respect to John Colgrove who farmed Poplars' Farm. Yes, John was paid for the land, but, without his willingness to help the village by making it available, Brickhill would still be waiting for its playing field today.

The 'new' pavilion later erected on the field was really anything but. Fred West, the father of builder Paul, mentioned earlier, and his younger brother Jeremy, spotted an advertisement in one of the local papers which said that Maulden Bowls Club, near Ampthill, was looking to dispose of its Terrapin-building pavilion. Alroy Pickersgill and Fred persuaded the firm of Anstee and Lawson at Woburn Sands to lend them one of their coal lorries and off they went to Maulden to do a deal.

Helpers at a 1980s Brickhill show take a well earned breather. Left to right: May Butcher, Madge Ellement, Joan Varney, Sharon Giles, Ron Varney.

They soon had the building dismantled, loaded on the lorry and back to Brickhill, where it was stored temporarily on the playing field in an old tin shed. Then, together with eight more Terrapin units obtained from the British Rail Social Club in Bletchley, Alroy, Fred, Maurice Tyler and a whole host of willing helpers set to and created Brickhill's 'new' pavilion.

By this time Bow Brickhill's village show was off the ground and the playing field was put to good use on show days. Just about the whole village seemed to lend a hand, from Mike and Chris Dickins, Robert Dimsdale and Maurice and Gladys Hitchins at the top of the hill, to Ken Burton and his family from Parkway, Alroy and Ann, Kenneth Lee and his family, the Parsons family, Derek and Meryl Sinfield and Dave and May Butcher from farther down Station Road, to name but just a few. The shows luckily seemed blessed with fine weather and I particularly remember one hilarious afternoon when we had a troop of donkeys shipped in for a Donkey Derby Day.

The next year, 1976, saw work going on apace on the field's cricket square to improve its playing surface. Again, it was drainage that was causing problems. Audrey Odell, the wife of Parish Council chairman Fred Odell, retired after 29 years as clerk to the council and Harold Barker, who lived in Woburn Sands but was the village roadman – lengthsman was his proper title – and who kept the paths, edges and gutters as clean as a new pin, also called it a day after 37 years. Those paths, edges and gutters have never looked the same since, particularly those along the Woburn Sands road.

The village just never seemed to be still at that time, for, if we were not planning the show, we were organising dances and dinners held at the Wavendon Community Centre or jumble sales and coffee mornings in various homes, at the pavilion or in the Church Hall. I think I must have worn a groove in the path to Ken Burton's house over the years, for there was always something to sort out.

Often Ken wouldn't be in, but be with his father, Jack, on a small piece of land they worked in London End Lane. 'Is he in?' I would ask Ken's wife, Enid, or one of the children. 'Up the chickens!' I would be told, meaning that Ken was tending their flock of hens on the London End ground. Ken Burton died in 1992 and we used to call him Sir Alf, after Sir Alf Ramsey who was the national team manager when England won the World Cup in 1966. But the footballing tradition lives on in the family. Odette, Ken and Enid's eldest daughter, is currently the Bow Brickhill club secretary and Girl Friday. Barbara and I called in to see her recently and there, on the line, were the team shirts, washed and drying and waiting to be ironed before Brickhill's next game. Ken followed his father, Jack, on to the Parish Council and Odette followed Ken in 1992.

By 1976 my work in London meant the time for committee work locally was lessening and so I resigned as chairman of the Sports and Social Club. At the 1976 annual dinner held at Wavendon, I was

Taking the strain at a Brickhill show in the mid-1980s. Left to right are: Colin Stone, Mark Pickersgill, John Battams, Geoge Battams, Trevor Cullip and Paul Hedges.

presented with an engraved silver paper knife which is still in daily use. I handed over the reins to the vice-chairman, Peter Jefferies, who then lived in the former Plough pub premises on Church Road, but something must have gone drastically wrong somewhere for within a year or so the Sports and Special club had collapsed, the various sections fragmented, and the only aspect left with any formal stature was the football side, still going today.

Two years on, in 1978, youngsters at the school celebrated its centenary, while at the other end of the age spectrum a 'Tuesday club' was formed for, shall we say, those with a few more years behind them but who were still young at heart! One of their first outings was a boat trip on the canal.

In 1983 Fred Odell resigned after 47 years service on the Parish Council, many of them as chairman, his retirement coming as Bow

Children at Bow Brickhill school for its centenary celebrations in 1978. At the back, left to right, are Janet Baker, Joan Wagstaff, headteacher Geoff Tremayne and Rosemary Walduck.

Brickhill began to feel the effects of its proximity to Milton Keynes, as did many other villages in the area. Traffic flows through the village increased rapidly, particularly during the 'rush-hour' periods, and a petition was presented to the Parish Council concerning the danger from cars on Church Road. Next year, 1984, the cricket team played its first league match on a well prepared table on the playing field.

In 1985 the village asked Bucks County Council to reduce the speed limit through the village but the request was turned down. The same year, All Saints church celebrated its 800th anniversary and around this time the Brickhills' Cup, a competition involving football sides from, Bow, Great and Little Brickhill, came into being, with Bow being the first winners. Village life, however, did seem gradually to be on the wane, or at least village life as many of us at the time remembered it. By 1988 the remaining village store and post office had closed down, so other than The Wheatsheaf pub and a pony trekking centre, the established commercial outlets had gone; no shop, no post office and, of course, no working farms. Even the older folks' Tuesday Club fell by the wayside.

Prior to Bow Brickhill's first league game of cricket in 1984 are, left to right, back row, Charlie Parsons, Jim Ivens, Stuart Leeming, Paul Hedges, Pete Russell, Tub Curruthers, Paul West; front row: Alroy Pickersgill, Bill Powrie, Danny Walters, Joe Carter jnr, Stephen Ward, Kate Carter.

The Bow Brickhill football team of the early 1980s in their sponsored shirts. Left to right, back row: Ken Burton, Andy Hale, Mark Pickersgill, Nick Cook, Mark Enever, Bill Powrie, Pete Russell, Pete Holland; front row: Pete Bamfield, Keith Holland, Colin Lee, Paul Hedges, Mitch Cronin, Nigel Helms, Alroy Pickersgill.

In 1986 Alroy Pickersgill hired Luton Town's ground for a football match on its artificial turf between his customers and the Bow Brickhill village side. Watching, from left, are Ken Burton, Libby West, Odette Holland and Ann Pickersgill.

Like so many other similar communities of the day and age, Bow Brickhill became a dormitory village. Even the school faced closure because of falling rolls, but, after a hard struggle, was eventually reprieved. The 1990s, however, brought some signs of a resurgence. A new village store was opened, though not destined to last all that long, Milton Keynes Development Corporation promised more than £200,000 towards the cost of a new pavilion for the playing field – and a handsome building it now is – and in late 1994 the Parish Council held an exhibition to mark its centenary.

The late 1990s saw the Brickhill show still an annual feature and Christine and Douglas Loak reviving the old Tuesday Club under a new name, the Bow Brickhill Club. In October 1999 the initial meeting attracted nine people but membership is now in excess of 40 and the club, which meets in the pavilion on the first Tuesday of each month, has a varied programme of outings and visiting speakers.

Football crazy! Jubilation in the mid-1980s when Bow Brickhill won the first playing of the Brickhills Cup.

Bow Brickhill Club members experience the London Eye on a visit to the capital.

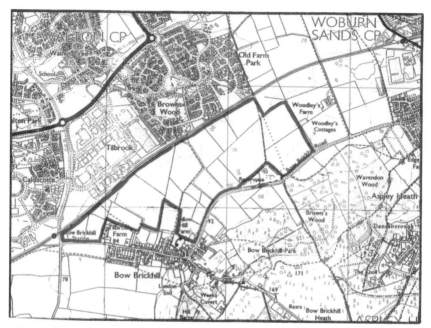

The possible expansion of Bow Brickhill towards the railway line outlined on a map of the area.

By the time we slipped into the new century, Milton Keynes had grown, as was planned, right up to Bow Brickhill's doorstep. The once open space between the railway crossing and Caldecote hamlet is now the very modern and completed Tilbrook industrial area. The spot where I clashed heads playing football and broke my tooth is now part of the carriageway of Brickhill Street. The open fields of the early 1970s are now the residential areas of Walnut Tree, Browns Wood, Old Farm Park and Caldecote. Even the course of the river, with its stepping stones where the children played on warm afternoons, has been altered to make way for Caldecote's balancing lake. And waiting in the wings there may be further changes.

In October 2000, Bow Brickhill learned that there were moves afoot by a dozen or so landowners to develop the Bow Brickhill end of the corridor of still open land between the railway line at Bow Brickhill and the Woodley's Farm area at Woburn Sands. Some 1450 new houses are proposed, so I believe, complete with shops, a new school and medical facilities. The scheme's viability relies on all the dozen or so landowners involved agreeing and signing up – and not all agree.

At the time of writing the proposals seem to be on hold but have led to the setting up of the PBB – the Preserve Bow Brickhill group. Many people in the village do not want to see more houses creeping beyond the original Milton Keynes boundary, in this case the railway line, and if the development does go ahead I believe it would be the first major building scheme to break through the boundary of the original designated area. Others, however, query what is there now worth preserving in Bow Brickhill; there is no shop, no post office, no local mobile tradesman anymore, only the church, a pub and the houses. Even the woodland areas are not as they were years ago, now that the golf courses are there.

This faction would clearly welcome the development which would bring, supposedly, shops, a doctor's surgery, perhaps a new school and above all, a post office at least, back to the neighbourhood. Certainly our current deputy prime minister, John Prescott, wants to see more houses built on the outskirts of Milton Keynes, so making the overall development much bigger than planned. But whether that overall policy is correct is very debatable, to say the least. To use that oldest of cliches: only time will tell.

CHAPTER 4

WOBURN SANDS AND ASPLEY GUISE

As Woburn Sands faced the prospect in 1970 of a new city on its doorstep, the community's major employer, Plysu, based in expanding premises opposite the Recreation Ground in Station Road, was floated on the Stock Exchange, with shares offered at nine shillings and sixpence (47.5p) which quickly rose to 86p. Decimal currency, I should point out, was introduced in 1971.

The founders of Plysu, Rohan Sturdy, left, and James Summerlin.

"Same with me – I find these thick PVC macs beautifully warm!"

A cartoon extolling the virtues of Plysu's wares by cartoonist Jack Mulroy. Jack and his wife and children lived in Church Road, Bow Brickhill, for some years before moving to Aspley Heath.

Co-founders Rohan Sturdy and James Summerlin had begun the business – as 'manufacturers, moulders, fabricators and merchants of plastic goods and materials of all types and descriptions' – in 1945 after meeting each other whilst carrying out their wartime work. They set up an office in a bombed-out house in Virginia Water, Surrey and, shortly after, high frequency welding to produce sponge bags, baby pants and other sheet vinyl products was done from a former Lloyds Bank building in Egham High Street.

In the summer of 1947, however, Plysu – the name comes from the code word for the wartime Government's Ministry of Supply – came to Woburn Sands, James Summerlin's wife's grandfather leaving them a small factory building on the corner of Station Road and The Grove.

My Aunt Violet, the wife of my father's eldest brother, Jim, was among Plysu's early recruitment of staff, for the family – I have two cousins, Frances and Bob – lived in The Grove, only yards away from the factory. Throughout the 1950s and 1960s the company saw both good and bad times and in the 1960s had the late and very famous comedian Les Dawson on its books as a salesman. I'm not suggesting that this brilliant comic was the cause of any great hardship, but he was fired for being an unsuccessful representative!

In 2000 the company was bought by Nampac, a South African organisation, and now trades under this name, though still operating from the Woburn Sands premises. Long before this, however, in 1964, Mike Dickins joined the company as product design manager, a role he continues to carry out to this day. Mike made Bow Brickhill his home in 1967 when he and his wife, Chris, moved to a house which they had built at the top of Bow Brickhill's steep hill on the former site of some cottages which stood at right-angles to the road. They lived there for almost ten years before moving to their present home in Mill Way, Aspley Guise.

During his many years with the company Mike has seen the organisation expand from its single plant at Woburn Sands to have several factories in the UK and, in addition, several small specialist plants set up on the premises of major customers such as the larger dairy chains who use the Plysu-Nampac containers for milk.

Mike played an important role in the design and development of what was known in the trade as the F80 bottle. Originally used as an orange squash container in the 1970s it did not sell well initially, because housewives were used to buying their squash in thick glass bottles which made the contents appear to be more than they were. The new plastic bottle made it look as if housewives were being sold short

James Summerlin, seated centre, with recipients of Plysu's long service awards in 1974. Back row, left to right: Barbara Woods, Jim Holden, Johnny Walker, Ursula Charnock-Smith, Peggy Inkpin, Cliff Atkinson, Mr Kenny, Kath Lane, Claude Phillips, Shiela Goodman, Jack Cable, Margaret Woods, Mary Robinson, John Eastaff. Front row: Vi Enever, May Nicholls, Joan Brawn, Hazel Rann, Kath Murray, V.Holmes, W.O'Sullivan, V.Garner, Molly Woollett, Mrs Garner.

measures! But this had changed by the 1980s when plastic containers were considered the norm, and by 1983 Plysu were producing a four-pint bottle that would stand in the door of a domestic 'fridge. Four years later there was another breakthrough when the company led the way with a five-litre container, known as the multiguard, which was used by the agrochemical market.

Always conscious of its responsibilities to its staff, Plysu was happy to recognise Trades Union representation early in its life, and its conditions of service and general friendly atmosphere meant that there were lots more local people who, like Mike Dickins, were to spend many working years with the firm.

Among these was the former personnel officer, Claude Phillips, who joined Plysu in 1953, initially as stores keeper before becoming welfare officer and then personnel officer. Sadly, Claude died some years ago but he was highly thought of in the community and was a man of great

In 1972 Claude Phillips, right, presents his shield to Plysu's top fisherman, Jack Sorrenson, centre, who in turn presents his youth challenge cup to the son of Plysu employee Dave Caton. Caton junior landed an 8lb carp to take the cup.

compassion, frequently visiting the sick either in their homes or in hospital and, if the latter, often driving their relatives to visit because of distances involved, for the nearest hospitals for the area prior to the opening of Milton Keynes hospital in the 1980s were at Bedford, Luton, Aylesbury and Northampton.

The social side of life at Plysu was also very important and by the 1970s the firm had a football side playing in the North Bucks league, a strong fishing club – there are excellent ponds on the works site – while the children of employees were given swimming lessons during the summer in the pool at James Summerlin's house in Aspley Guise, and the works canteen was the venue for many in-house functions as well as being used at Christmas for the annual party for local old age pensioners.

Close links were also forged over the years with the County fire service for most of its volunteer firemen at Woburn Sands worked at Plysu, literally just across the road from the fire station. Shrewd businessman that he was, it hadn't escaped Rohan Sturdy's notice that it was no bad thing to have trained firemen on your staff when you're running a plastics factory!

Frank Todd gives swimming lessons to youngsters in James Sumerlin's pool in 1973. The children are, left to right: Mark Thurston, Stewart Ikin, Stewart Copeland, Diane Langridge, James Bayliss, Gary Leadbeater, Angela Hill, Andrea Tucker, Julie Copeland, Elaine Murdoch, Susan Voss, Wendy Voss, Susan Passenham, Stephanie Voss.

The Plysu firemen at practice, led by Wally Wade in the white helmet. Also pictured are Brian Rogers, Keith Leadbeater, Don Hill and Brian Griffin.

*At the Plysu
Christmas party
for the old folks
of Woburn Sands
in 1972, Mrs J.
Summerlin is
pictured with an
award-winning
cake. Also, left to
right, are: Ken
Coleman, Dora
Buckthorpe,
Midge Hollier
and Audrey
Britten.*

Rohan Sturdy retired to the Bahamas in the mid-1970s, but James Summerlin carried on as company chairman until his retirement in 1995. Both are now deceased, but they have left behind them a company with a special place in the heart of Woburn Sands.

Of course, and as I have mentioned in Chapter 1, other even longer established businesses have provided local employment, with the brickyards at Brogborough and Newton Longville, plus the railway, offering jobs over many years. But railway cutbacks, automated processes and privatisation under the last Conservative Government in the early 1990s have reduced manpower in this industry, while North Bucks as a whole has lost its important position as a major brick making area with the closure over the last fifteen years of the yards at both Brogborough, in the early 1980s, and Newton Longville only two or three years later.

For Woburn Sands and Aspley Guise pollution from the brickworks was a daily occurrence in the past. When the wind was in a certain quarter, wherever you went in Bletchley and out in the villages towards Bedford, you could almost taste the sulphur fumes, so bad was it at times. But though the brickworks have now gone, and with them that particular pollution problem, environmentalists in the two communities of Woburn Sands and Aspley Guise, and in neighbouring Woburn, found

The Edgebury convalescent home on Aspley Heath, demolished to make way for apartment homes in 1988.

themselves faced with an additional problem in the 1970s, one which has, perhaps – and I use the word 'perhaps' very carefully – only recently been resolved. It was the mining of Fullers Earth, a mineral now used widely in the paper making industry and an operation which changed the face of large tracts of land which, for years, Woburn Sands and Aspley residents have called 'the woods'.

The firm of Steetley Bentonite began is first extraction of Fullers Earth from Woburn Sands as far back as 1952 when mining took place in the Tidbury wooded area just off The Leys. The mineral was being extensively used in the foundry industry at the time, with car manufacturers among the major customers; Volvo, for example, took hundreds of tons. Work at the site continued until 1958, when it was closed down, but it soon opened again and mineral extraction did not finish there until 1961.

John Hill, the young son of the works manager, worked there during his school holidays and remembers how, during the 1950s, a great deal of testing was carried out in the woods to determine how much of the mineral lay beneath the surface. By the end of the decade a major find of more than a million tons was located under Aspley woods, planning permission to excavate was given, and the site opened in 1961 with an entrance off what, as a boy, I remember as Birchmoor Lane, now known more commonly, I believe, as Aspley Lane. The material was sent to London Colney for processing and the prediction was that there was enough Fullers Earth there to give the company 25 years of work.

Accordingly, the Hill family moved to Woburn – 23 Bedford Street, next door to The Bell pub, to be precise – and young John began working for the company in 1962 on what was intended to be a short-term basis. Driving dumper trucks and heavy plant made the job a boyhood dream, he says, and some 41 years later, he is still there, but now as works manager.

The Steetley works as it is today began its life in the very bad winter of 1962–63 when it began snowing at Christmas and there was still snow on the ground and sub-zero temperatures the following March. But the works meant that processing the mineral on site could now be done, so saving the haul to London Colney.

As output from the site increased there were problems with large lorries getting in and out of Aspley Lane. Planning permission for an entrance to the works off the main Woburn–Woburn Sands road was sought by the company in 1963 but was not granted until 1972. It was only then that the entrance used today was opened up. In the following year, 1974, planning permission was sought to open operations on the other side of the Woburn road, where more large deposits had been found in the late 1960s in the Aspley Heath and Bow Brickhill wooded areas.

But opposition to the extent of Steetley's mining operation was by now growing apace as the local communities protested that the amenity value of the woods for walking and admiring in a natural state was being denied them. These concerns played a major part in the planning application being turned down at a public inquiry. However, the company won the day when the refusal was overturned by the Department of the Environment on the grounds that a comparatively

The road bridge across the Woburn Road to serve the Steetley site, pictured in 1985.

rare indigenous mineral was available.

As the deposits from these later sites were extracted, a further eyesore – at least in the eyes of the local community – came into view in 1977 with the building of a traffic bridge over the Woburn road. The bridge gave direct access to the processing works from the site, which had a life expectancy into the 1990s. However, in the late 1980s the company was visited by the Minerals Planning Authority to investigate possible deposits lying under the Woburn road itself.

The result was that once more the cycle of a Steetley planning application to extract from under the road and in the process altering the line of the road, followed by refusal followed by public inquiry, was entered into, with the Woburn Sands Society at the forefront of the environmental objections. At the public inquiry it was clear there was a very fine balance between the environmental factors and the need for the mineral, but the mineral won the day. In truth, there were parts of the Woburn road slightly to the south of the works entrance which curved somewhat and were overshadowed by high sandstone bluffs.

Trees come down to make way for the diversion of the Woburn road in 1992.

Pretty to look at, yes, but with the increasing traffic of the day, not always the safest place to find yourself when behind the wheel of a vehicle. A time limit of only six months was imposed on Steetley to realign the road – what we would now call a planning gain – and work began in March 1993.

By late autumn the road was open to traffic and within a day of the opening, trees were being felled adjacent to the old road line to get at the Fullers Earth deposits. Production began in November with the site having a life expectancy of ten years. Within a year a new processing mill capable of better grading was installed at the works to meet the wants of the paper industry, now taking almost all of Steetley's product but demanding a finer grade.

Steetley then made a further planning application to mine the Wavendon Heath south area – what we, locally, know as Longslade – but the application was refused by Beds County Council. The subsequent public inquiry upheld the County Council decision but in February of this year (2003) Steetley went to the High Court to appeal.

The new road open to traffic in the winter of 1992.

The very last load taken from the Aspley Heath mining sites in 1992. The depth of the excavations dwarf the large dumper truck and digger.

The company lost the case. So, with those ten years of work on the old road site now up, and having lost the case in the High Court, John Hill told me recently that he does not know what the future holds for Steetley at Woburn Sands. Many of his workforce, he says, have been with him many, many years and there is now a large question mark over any future mining operations.

However, this is good news for the environmental campaigners serving on Beds County Council's liaison committee and the organisation known as The Campaign to Protect Woburn and District from Open Cast Mining. Working closely together, the two bodies have kept a watching brief on the Steetley operations. A member of the County liaison committee is Dr David Parkins, born and bred in Woburn Sands, and who represents the Woburn Sands Society. He feels that at long last there is a good chance that the woods will be returned to the community for their leisure use and points out that the company said many years ago that excavated sites would be rehabilitated so that in ten years the woodland areas used in its operations would be back to normal. But that hasn't happened, for the simple reason that, although Steetley has carried out much replanting of trees, and low growing vegetation such as heathers are regenerating, you can't get a ten year old tree to look the same as the 80-years-old specimen that came out and it is attempting to replace. John Hill told me he fully understands the local concerns and, when David Parkins and I met with him earlier this year, I was impressed with the way both men were able to talk frankly, but amiably, about both sides of the argument.

Like the management of Steetley, David Parkins is also unsure of what the future might hold. Born in the same road as he now lives – Downham Road in Woburn Sands – in 1932, David attended Aspley Heath school and remembers me being introduced to his class in 1940. That was when I came to Woburn Sands with my parents after losing our London home on the first night of the German blitz in the Second World War.

From Aspley Heath David moved on to Wolverton Grammar, did his two years National Service with the RAF from 1950–52, and then worked in the research department at Stewartby brick works for the next four years. Spells with the Aircraft Research Association, Hunting Engineering at Ampthill and Allen's, of Bedford, led up to him joining Cranfield Institute of Technology – now Cranfield University – in 1971. In 1976 he gained his Ph.D. and continued at Cranfield until he retired as senior lecturer in 1997. For the last eleven years of his working life Dr Parkins had his own group undertaking research into fluid film lubrication. He is now a consultant and private tutor.

So, what the future will hold for the centuries old woodland of the Woburn Sands district no-one quite knows, now that Steetley have been refused further planning permissions by Beds County Council. But one thing is certain. David Parkins and his fellow environmentalists will be keeping a wary eye on those lists of planning applications...

One planning application that did bring enormous benefit to both Woburn Sands and Aspley Guise, however, was that which saw the building of the Asplands medical centre in Wood Street, Woburn Sands, in 1982. There is now a distinct 'health care' ambiance to this area, for in close proximity are the medical centre, a retirement home and Ken Adam's dental surgery.

In the early 1980s, solicitor Michael Kemp, now retired and living at Aspley Guise, owned a land-locked parcel of ground whose westerly end was bordered by land with a frontage to Wood Street and owned by Milton Keynes Council. At that time Woburn Sands, Aspley Guise and Woburn each had their own resident doctor. For Aspley it was Doctor Warden with a surgery in School Lane, now known as Woburn Lane, which was just beyond the D.C.Hall light engineering works though on the other side of the road. Doctor David Rhodes looked after Woburn Sands with a surgery in bungalow premises in Station Road, leased from Plysu, and Doctor Barnes was in Woburn. Plysu's expansion plans at the time, though, showed no future for the surgery in Station Road, so Doctor Rhodes put forward a case to Milton Keynes Borough Council for a combined medical centre. The Council was enthusiastic and the

The Remembrance Day service in Woburn Sands in November 1979.

end result was that the three surgeries combined to make the current practice now in operation, headed by Doctor John Logan, who took over from Doctor Rhodes, ably assisted meantime by Doctors Nott and Rogers and all working from the purpose-built centre in Wood Street.

About a third of the building was on Council land, the remainder on Michael Kemp's ground. At the same time this unlocked the rest of the site for the development of bungalows which now stand on what we know as Asplands Close. Both medical centre and close take their name from an amalgamation of parts of the names of the two villages whose histories are so closely linked.

With a growing Milton Keynes providing many opportunities for work, Woburn Sands and Aspley Guise have suffered little in the way of unemployment as local commercial bases have gone by the board. Some of these I will mention later in this chapter but, with Woburn Sands having enjoyed town status now for some years, there is some disagreement being voiced about plans to move its civic offices from the southern end of the High Street to a site further north nearer the station.

Pupils from Bury Lawn School, Aspley Heath, present Harvest Festival gifts in September 1985 to a group of Woburn Sands pensioners. Pictured are Mrs Jessie Robinson, Mrs Doris King and Mrs Florence Robinson receiving the gifts from Paul Cheeseman and Peggy Waller.

Woburn Sands is still expanding, for currently houses are being built close to the railway crossing and some 300 new homes are scheduled for former Plysu land off Station Road. At the time of writing the Town Council offices are housed in an extension built to the Ellen Pettit Memorial Hall in the High Street, the hall constructed in 1928 from monies left to the parish church, St Michael's, by Mr A.W. Pettit with the wish that a hall be built in memory of his wife, Ellen. The hall was erected within the large grounds of St Michael's vicarage. With no money left in trust to run the hall and associated land, it was sold in January 1970 by the church to Newport Pagnall Rural District Council.

Woburn Sands Parish Council applied for a loan to purchase the hall and build an extension the following year and this move led to the Rural Council dividing the complete plot into three, the first part being the hall and proposed extension, which was bought by the Parish Council; the second the vicarage itself, which was converted to business use and is now known as Shelton House; and the remainder kept for the

The rear of the Ellen Pettit hall in Woburn Sands comes down to make way for a new extension to be used by the Town Council.

building of Shelton Court, the sheltered accommodation and its gardens, which are still in the ownership of the local authority.

In 1990 Woburn Sands Town Council, as it had now become, extended the rear of the hall into a meeting room and office for its own use and this new extension was formally opened in April of that year. The Council was later approached by the owners of Shelton House to see if they might purchase the hall so that Shelton House might be expanded, but the Council made it clear that it would not wish to sell the hall unless an alternative venue could be found which would be an improvement on existing facilities. The former Plysu site, now owned by Nampac, is due to be developed as I have mentioned earlier, and the Town Council, as part of that planning gain, will be given the former Plysu Sports and Social Club, with land. Planning permission has now been granted for the Ellen Pettit Memorial Hall to be converted to offices but when this was announced at the Woburn Sands Town Council's annual meeting in April 2002, a parish meeting was requested

The Woburn Sands band parade at a Christmas lights switch-on in the early 1990s.

to discuss the issue and a 'Save our Hall' group was formed by some local residents. The parish meeting went ahead in July 2002 and a parish poll was legally requested, making perhaps a little piece of special local government history for Woburn Sands.

The poll took place on 23 July 2002 and out of 1849 electorates, 372 voted that the hall should not be sold and 260 voted for the change to take place, a 31 per cent turnout. As a parish poll is not legally binding, the Town Council at its next meeting chose to disregard the voting pattern and go ahead with the sale. It is expected that the Council will be in its new home by the end of this year (2003) and monies made from the sale of the Ellen Pettit hall will be used to refurbish and upgrade facilities at the Institute, the Council's other public hall on the corner of the High Street and Chapel Street. The new hall on the Plysu/Nampac site will also be upgraded and the local playgroup have already expressed an interest to move there.

There is one other hiccup of Woburn Sands life that I think it worth

The Phoenix club stall at the festivities to mark a Christmas lights switch-on in Woburn Sands in the early 1990s.

recording, albeit because it perhaps comes from an unlikely source – the Women's Institute. In 1988 membership of the Woburn Sands WI was falling away and some felt this was because of the way the county organisation of the movement was being handled at the time. The Woburn Sands branch consequently disbanded, but from its ashes rose a new women's group, the Phoenix Club. Initially the club prospered, but as original members passed away or found meetings difficult to attend, the club found itself unable to continue. No officers could be found at the annual meeting on 15 May 1996, so the club was disbanded.

The changing times have also brought about the demise of many businesses in the two villages, as I mentioned earlier, and these include two in Aspley Guise synonymous with life for more than 100 years. They were the printers known as The Powage Press and the family butchers, Barnwells.

Begun in Woburn in 1872 by the grandfather of the retired solicitor Michael Kemp, whom I have already mentioned, 'the Powage', as it quickly became known, moved to its Salford Road premises in 1875. The company prospered and to have a tradesman's job there or to be taken on as an apprentice was quite a feather in your cap. Michael's father and mother, Charles Minter Kemp and Ella Kemp, lived at The Haven, a house at the top of the hill at Bow Brickhill where their neighbours were Mr and Mrs Long, who were both schoolteachers, and Mr Harvey, an eminent barrister. Michael's father duly took over from his father as managing director of Powage Press but in 1966 it was sold on to the Vernon family. However, the business did not do well at this stage, so in 1972 the Kemps bought it back. By the turn of the century, though, plant and equipment was sold off and The Powage Press ceased to exist. The property, however, is still owned by the family, though now leased out, and I believe some aspects of the print trade are still carried on from there.

From 1973–79 Michael Kemp served on Aspley Guise Parish Council, the last two years as chairman. He describes Aspley as being a quiet village in the early 1970s with the middle of the decade seeing the Parish Council bringing benefits to the children of the Trunk Furlong estate in Salford Road by providing a recreation ground, called Townlands.

A small playground was created on land owned by the Council, play equipment was installed, an all-weather pitch put down and a shed appeared, courtesy of Wolverton Rugby Club. Elsewhere, some eyebrows were raised when the Council allowed tipping to take place on The Common, but in due course this not only tidied up its edges but extended the public area.

The other long established business that has gone is that of Barnwell's, the family butchers, founded in the late 1800s by James Brandon Barnwell, a butcher in nearby Eversholt where he was in partnership with his three brothers. James moved to Aspley Guise about this time and opened up his own premises on the corner of Spinney Lane and Mount Pleasant. The business was handed on from father to son and I remember, as a boy, Frank Barnwell running the enterprise. Frank and his wife were very accomplished old-tyme dancers and seldom missed a dance at Aspley's Parish Hall.

Frank handed on to his son, Reg, who ran the business in partnership with two other members of the family, Clem and George. This three-handed partnership broke up and the business was run solely by Reg who was joined in the late 1960s by his sons, Gary and Clive, the two boys being the great, great, great grandsons of James Barnwell, the Eversholt butcher.

When the Second World War ended in 1945, Frank, Clem and Reg were given authority to establish a slaughterhouse on site, but new legislation covering slaughtering in later years meant changes had to be made to the building. It was duly modernised, almost doubled in size, and with the changing patterns of family shopping brought about by the supermarkets, the slaughtering side led the business to move into the wholesale market in the 1970s. Clive tells me that again the legislation covering trading was lengthy and complex.

That side of the business did well, however, and it soon became clear that the Mount Pleasant premises were not big enough to handle the volume of work being created. Reg died in 1981, leaving the two younger men to carry through plans for expansion which they achieved by buying a smallholding at Hanslope. Slaughtering on site in Aspley had presented a variety of problems for their residential neighbours, not least the number of lorries associated with both collection and delivery, so the move to Hanslope left the shop as a retail unit with a dwindling customer base.

In 1986 Gary and Clive decided to concentrate solely on the wholesale side and the shop was closed, ultimately demolished, and mews-style houses built on the site. By the turn of the century the wholesale business was sold on and more than a hundred years of family trading by the Barnwells had come to an end. The family, though, is still connected with Aspley, for Clive and his wife Barbara live at number 4 Mount Pleasant, a bungalow first owned by his grandfather, Frank, but now refurbished and extended.

The original Barnwell butcher's shop in Mount Pleasant, Aspley Guise, above, and below, the rebuilt premises in the 1980s.

The Barnwell staff in 1980. Included are Lyn White, Norma Rogers, Clarice Dudley, Denis Foster, Reg, Gary and Clive Barnwell, Greg Cox and the young man at the front, a member of the Greenhood family.

In Aspley Guise now the biggest change you will notice from the 1970s is the number of vehicles that clog every one of its thoroughfares. It is not unique in this respect, of course, for the car now dominates our lives and the houses and roads of Aspley Guise were not built with such vast volumes of traffic in mind. But the car has brought us a personal mobility undreamt of by earlier generations and it is that mobility, as I have mentioned before, that has hastened the demise of many tradesmen and businesses in rural communities. However, it has brought benefits to newer enterprises, and in Aspley, the hotel and restaurant Moore Place, formerly The Holt, falls into this category.

As I have written in the two earlier volumes of this trilogy, The Holt dominates Aspley's Square and was used as a Land Army hostel during the Second World War. Later the home of Fred Wright, by the 1970s it was being run as a village hostelry by Len Beswick and his wife, and it

The Holt, soon to be renamed Moore Place, undergoes its facelift in 1987.

was Len who opened its highly successful cellar bar. It became a favourite watering hole of my father, who supplied fresh produce from his allotments to both the Barnwell shop in Mount Pleasant, to sell on, and to Len Beswick for catering purposes. Money might not have changed hands but I think father was duly rewarded either with excellent steak or a pint or two of his favourite tipple!

Built by Frances Moore in 1786 during the reign of George III, The Holt celebrated its bi-centenary by standing empty. However, refurbishment plans were afoot and with work carried out by the Bletchley based Weathercock Properties, a £2.5 million facelift saw the premises opened on 1 February 1988 under its present name, Moore Place, and boasting 54 en-suite bedrooms under the banner of a country house hotel. Only last year its continuing success saw an additional ten bedrooms added when a listed cottage on West Hill, and adjacent to the present hotel car park, was brought into the complex.

During the Second World War and the 1950s, I remember the cottage being the surgery of Doctor Richardson, the village GP.

In 1991, while working for Milton Keynes Development Corporation, I used the hotel's conference rooms for business meetings. Its murder mystery dinners, jazz dinners and summer ball are all popular events and, though I haven't eaten in its award winning Greenhouse Restaurant, my son and daughter-in-law have, and speak very highly of it. The hotel is privately owned and a member of the Best Western and Johanssen Group.

At one time Aspley Guise boasted many public houses and these included The Steamer, just outside The Square towards the foot of West Hill, and The Duke's Head, which stood on the corner of West Hill and Duke Street. I confess throughout my long association with the village I can only remember three, before Len Beswick opened The Holt. They were The Anchor and The Bell, in The Square, and The Wheatsheaf, in Mount Pleasant.

Both The Anchor and The Bell are still there, although very recently The Bell, built in 1837, was refurbished and moved from pub to restaurant status. It now trades under the name of Aspley's Restaurant. At The Anchor, my father played darts for the pub for several years when the licensee was Maurice Hall. Its present day pub lunches are good, and I best remember The Bell for the Friday night skittle games I played in its back room during the 1950s and '60s. The Wheatsheaf, nearest to our long since demolished family home in Mount Pleasant, was the pub where I was introduced in the 1950s to what was then every young man's first drink, a bottle of light ale. It was kept then by Mrs Amy Long and was looked upon by my grandfather, who lived with us, almost as his personal retreat. He was a good dominoes and crib player and I remember him telling me one very cold winter's day that he might be cold getting to The Wheatsheaf, but he knew he wouldn't feel the cold coming back!

In 1978, eleven years after my grandfather had said farewell to life at the age of 87, Bill and Ann Cox, both well known locally, moved into The

Front and rear views of Moore Place after its upgrading.

Wheatsheaf. Bill was born and raised in nearby Salford, Ann 'up the hill' as they say in next door Cranfield. They were married in 1959 and during the 1960s both worked for Woburn Sands businessman Rob Harris, who ran Pikesley's Garage. Ann worked in the office, keeping the books, Bill in the garage as a mechanic.

Their foray as publicans was to last for 21 years, all at The Wheatsheaf, and their fund raising for charity during that time amounted to more than £43,000. Not for nothing was The Wheatsheaf dubbed 'the pub with the Midas touch'!

After knuckling down to the routine of actually running the pub, Bill set to work on getting the garden to rights and making it virtually an extension to the bars. Then he and Ann decided to raise money for the elderly members of Aspley's Silver Threads club and the cash they quickly drew in gave the old folk a memorable day out in Brighton. Next they embarked on a pile of pennies to buy talking books for the blind and had former Aspley resident John Dankworth on hand to push the pile over.

From then on, they say, the good causes came thick and fast and over the years the charities and groups they raised money for included Aspley Guise cubs and scouts, the village playgroup and toddlers' group and guide dogs for the blind. Specific projects covered areas as diverse as holiday funds for the disabled and bikes for under privileged children, to specific items of medical equipment and beds for Stoke Mandeville hospital.

The events the pair organised to raise money were just as diverse. The round-the-pubs pram race quickly became an annual event, as did the Crawley brook race where a furniture van had to take all the race apparel from The Wheatsheaf, on through Mount Pleasant and all the way down Horsepool Lane to the brook. New Year's Day inevitably saw a football match.

The war memorial, on its Bedford Road site in Aspley Guise, was also the recipient of Wheatsheaf largesse, for when its main post rotted away and the memorial itself was left lying in the grass, it was Wheatsheaf

John Dankworth gets ready to push over the pile of pennies at The Wheatsheaf.

St Trinians's girls, above, and an evil-looking crew, below, get ready for a Wheatsheaf round-the-pubs race.

A competitor splashes his way through Crawley brook close to Horsepool Lane.

The Harrison family, plus willing helpers, take race apparel to Crawley brook for a Wheatsheaf race.

Bill and Ann Cox with some of their teapots.

Pictured during an Aspley Guise WI sponsored knit-in to raise funds in 1975 are, left to right: Mrs Ann Davey-Turner, Mrs Jean Martell and Mrs Margaret Rogers.

money that paid for the repair and restoration work in 1983. A small plaque at the base of the memorial recognises the pub's generosity.

Just as an aside, Ann began in her spare time to build up a sizeable collection of teapots – 253 at the last count and, no, there wasn't a lot of spare time – and the collection came to the notice of Anglia TV. A camera crew turned up at The Wheatsheaf and filmed a piece which went on air next evening. But in 1999 Bill and Ann decided to call it a day. They left The Wheatsheaf but didn't go very far, only as far, in fact, as number 51, Mount Pleasant, just up the road and the old home of Mrs Elsie Fowler, who for many years gave the children of Aspley Guise piano lessons. I was one of her pupils. Now Bill and Ann are semi-retired – Bill is 65 and Ann 64 – and work most mornings as jobbing gardeners. They look back on their Wheatsheaf days with much satisfaction but as they are both quick to point out, they could not have raised £43,000 without the support of their regular customers and the community at large.

As the millennium came into sight there was also good news for

The vicar of St Botolph's, Aspley Guise, really got the bird in 1978 – an emu. The Rev. Bob Hardie decided to take his feathered friend along to open the church fete in the grounds of Aspley House.

Aspley's scout troop, by now combined with Woburn Sands, for they opened their new headquarters on the site of the old bowling green in Spinney Lane, close to the Parish Hall.

After Geoff Hulance, from Salford Road and very well known in the village, and I restarted the troop in 1951, it continued to operate until 1989. Six years later, in 1995, it started up again, was duly amalgamated with the Woburn Sands troop and the combined organisation, with Steve Spicer from Bedford as scoutmaster, now boast 150 scouts, two cub packs of about 30 each, and 20 beavers. I don't think Geoff and I ever imagined scouting in the two villages would attract those sorts of numbers, but it's nice to know that great oaks from little acorns grow...

CHAPTER 5

MEDIA CHANGES AND REGENERATION

While Bletchley enjoyed its boom years of the early 1970s the new city area of Milton Keynes was being well served by several local newspapers and the then still comparatively new Anglia Television. Of the newspapers, the Wolverton Express commanded much respect in what is now referred to as north Milton Keynes; the eastern flank around Newport Pagnell and reaching as far a field as Olney was the province of the Bucks Standard, based in Newport Pagnell; the Woburn Reporter plied the Woburn, Woburn Sands and Aspley Guise areas, and for the west and south regions of the new Milton Keynes, the Bletchley District Gazette was essential weekend reading.

Though in the late 1960s the Bucks Standard had begun to embrace new technology, the Wolverton Express, Woburn Reporter and the Gazette kept to the traditional means of production, known in the newspaper world as 'hot metal'. This meant that all editorial and advertising material was produced by machines which stamped the impression of a letter or complete word into molten metal, which was then allowed to cool before being assembled by staff known as compositors to a pre-determined page design, called a lay-out. Once the page was assembled, it became known as a 'forme' and from the forme a paper-mache impression was taken which was the 'flong'. From this impression, the printing plate was ultimately produced, the plate went on to the press and the newspaper was duly 'run off' or, in layman's terms, printed.

In the late 1960s the Gazette moved from its Queensway offices to

Ward Road on the Mount Farm Estate, a move which allowed for the first time in many years all editorial, advertising and production staff to work under the same roof. Until then, all production work had been undertaken at two sites, one in Leighton Buzzard, where the type was set and the compositors worked, and the other at Luton, where, as part of the Home Counties Group controlled by the Gibbs family, the newspaper was printed.

At this time Carl Moser edited the Gazette, but within a year or two had left to join Milton Keynes Development Corporation to run its press office. He was succeeded by David Crewe, who in turn followed Carl to MKDC, and for a short while Graham Stewart-Reed held the editor's chair before making way for John Baker, who had been with the Gazette for some years as deputy-editor.

As the decade of the 1970s slipped away, the Gazette, which by now had changed its title to the Milton Keynes Gazette, was still in a healthy position. Its circulation had increased as Milton Keynes grid squares bordering Bletchley became populated and a 96-page paper was not unheard of. But it still stuck to its old production methods and, by its Luton management refusing to change editorial, advertising and production policies, it was eventually to lose out to a new player on the scene.

In 1965 a young Gordon Hart did what I did fourteen years earlier – he joined the Gazette as a junior reporter and under Carl Moser went through the same training ritual as I had experienced. Gordon's family came to Bletchley in 1955 from Lancashire, where he had been born seven years earlier, and his father, who worked in a cotton mill, was an accomplished classical and jazz violinist. This musical talent soon surfaced in Gordon who, by the age of five, was playing the ukulele. But journalism beckoned as a career and, though he kept up his musical studies by having piano lessons with Bletchley teacher, Arthur Hill, bought his first guitar at 11 and was playing local 'gigs' at the London Brick Company club in Selbourne Avenue by the time he was 14 – which his parents didn't know about until a neighbour who was there told them how good he was – it was the hooks, circles and strokes of shorthand outlines that began to dominate his working life at the Gazette. Gordon vividly recalls going to court with his chief reporter, Bill Clarke, in the mid-1960s and watching him in awe take down the proceedings with a really lightning fast shorthand note. But as Gordon was to learn, Bill, who lived in Water Eaton Road, was renowned for his shorthand skills.

Trevor Johnson and Gordon Hart met up as colleagues on the Gazette's editorial staff when Trevor took up full-time journalism at the age of 24. Living in Towcester and working at the Plessey electronics plant there, Trevor had for some years written angling notes, and other 'bits of copy' as he puts it, for the local press. So when the chance came to join the Gazette, he took it.

His particular patch of territory became the Tinkers Bridge, Coffee Hall, Netherfield and Beanhill areas and he recalls going to Netherfield after residents complained that their floors were moving. It was to be the start of the long running newspaper story of 'bouncing floors'. The houses, Trevor relates, were built with what were known as 'flexible floors' but following the complaints engineers carried out stress experiments to ensure they were safe. Trevor was inside one of the houses at the time and saw the floors bend through four inches before discretion became the better part of valour and he got out of the building quickly, just in case...

On another occasion he was sent to Loughton to see what life was like for some caravan dwellers living in the middle of a landscape dominated by the building of modern dwellings. As he pulled up in his car he clearly saw in one of the caravans a couple, shall we say, enjoying each other's company! They spotted Trevor and the gentleman quickly dressed, came out of the caravan at a high rate of knots and headed straight for him. Trevor half expected a punch on the nose or some verbal abuse at the very least, but the fellow ran straight past him without a word, jumped into a van, and tore off down the road! Somewhat perplexed, to say the least, Trevor was then confronted by the lady in question after, he insists, she had pulled on some clothes. 'Sorry about that, luv,' she told Trevor, 'but he thought you were me 'usband!'

Gordon, too, recalls the lighter moments, one being when he went out to the Brickhills where a Roman urn had been found. The prized artifact was put for safe keeping behind the driver's seat in a lorry, but when a new driver, a big fellow, took over, the first thing he did was to move the seat backwards to accommodate his large frame. The Gazette headline to Gordon's story was: 'History crushed in a second.'

In 1981 the new player appeared; it called itself the Milton Keynes Citizen and it threw away the established newspaper rule book.

My own teaching on the Gazette in the 1950s, and that experienced by both Gordon and Trevor in later years, was that the quality of editorial matter sold newspapers, and the more that were sold, the more that 'circulation', as it is called, could be used as a guarantee to current and potential advertisers that their products, services or jobs that were on offer would get to that number, or level, of people. The idea behind the Citizen was different but simple enough. Don't set out to sell papers; set out to give to advertisers their guarantee of a large circulation by giving papers away free! It was the enterprise of two men, Gerry West and Bill Alder, who were with the Luton Herald and Post.

With the Citizen delivered free through every door of a rapidly expanding Milton Keynes, the new newspaper was able to use this 'circulation' figure to poach advertisers away from the established journals in Milton Keynes while at the same time undercutting their advertising rates. Added to this two-pronged attack was the fact that the Citizen embraced new technology from day one and it contracted out the production side, so needing fewer people to take the newspaper forward. Eight members of staff – one reporter and seven on the advertising side – put the first edition together; the Gazette employed close on 50 to do the same weekly task.

The print run of the first issue of the Citizen was around 60,000 copies, dwarfing anything any of the established papers could offer. It

MILTON KEYNES Citizen

No. 1   October 1, 1981

Lots inside it — and it's FREE!

THIS is your first FREE copy of the Citizen, which will be delivered to 60,000 homes and businesses in and around the borough every Thursday.

Inside is you'll find news, sport, a full weekend television guide and details of what's on at cinemas in the area.

There's also a women's page, a prize crossword and a section devoted to children, including a free to enter competition.

And that's not all that's free. Do you want to clear those unwanted bits and pieces out of your home? You can advertise anything up to a value of £50 without paying. Just turn to the coupon on pages 14 and 25 and you're half-way to selling it.

The Citizen is always pleased to hear from its readers, no matter which part of its circulation area they come from. If you have an item of news for the paper then give us a ring on Milton Keynes 605544.

Enjoy looking through your Citizen and watch out for it again next Thursday.

EDITORIAL AND ADVERTISING TEL: MILTON KEYNES 605544

City firm hit

THIEVES made off with a £27,000 haul from a Bletchley warehouse last week.

They took a lorry loaded with pianos, organs, televisions and video recorders from J.L. of Hinchles (Keyboard Express) Ltd's premises in Barton Road.

Manager John Lutman, pictured, said the equipment was to a Dodge lorry waiting to go to East Anglia.

The lorry, registration number WYC 914S, contained 33 televisions, 29 organs, seven pianos and two video recorders.

All were brand new and in boxes.

BID TO BEAT M1 MANIACS

POLICE have issued a warning in a bid to beat the motorway maniacs.

Figures released this week show that since roadworks began on the M1 between the Milton Keynes turn-off and junction 13 in May there have been more than 80 crashes.

Nearly 40 people have been injured, 16 of them seriously. Now police are urging drivers to act cautiously to prevent death.

"With the bad weather not far off, we want motorists to remember how dangerous it can be," said a spokesman for Bedfordshire Police.

"When the frost and ice come it will be even worse."

Accidents

He said most of the accidents were caused by motorists driving carelessly as they approached the contra-flow system, in which for 2½ miles vehicles travel in both directions on one side of the road.

By FRASER PEARSON

slow down," he warned.

The contra-flow system was reversed last week as contractors A. Monk & Co. turned their attention to the southbound carriageway.

They are rebuilding the centre lane and resurfacing the centre and right-hand lanes as part of their £3.3 million contract. If all goes well, the work will be finished by December.

Drama

The motorway was the scene of drama — and another crash — early on Tuesday morning.

A Hillman Minx estate car crashed into a police Range Rover after a 15-minute 80mph chase.

"It appears that they are not prepared to lose time by getting into the correct lane when they should.

"They must pay attention to the road signs which give adequate advance warning of the contra-flow arrangement.

"Get into the proper lanes earlier enough and

It came to grief as the Woburn end of the roadworks and two men were arrested.

That's bloomin' odd . . .

It's flower power for Tom

THERE seems to be more bloom than boom about the anti-bomb business these days.

A van promoting nuclear protection systems was seen in Olney this week stuffed full of flowers.

Are flowers replacing fission?

"Not bloomin' likely, says Tom Butler, the man behind the company called Nuclear Protection.

"One of my other firms hires out artificial flowers. We use five vehicles for it and one has the nuclear message on the side to promote that part of my operation."

He said the vehicle that delivered nuclear protection equipment to people's homes was discreetly unmarked.

DJ Noel drops in

DISC jockey Noel Edmonds, pictured, dropped in on Milton Keynes on Saturday.

The radio and television star, famous for his jokes at the new city's expense, flew by helicopter from his home near Aylesbury to open a housing development in Downs Barn.

Noel's signature and flying machine proved to be popular attractions.

£500,000 DEAL

WE'RE with the Woolwich! That's what Milton Keynes Development Corporation are saying following a £½ million deal with the building society.

Under the agreement, the Woolwich will take over some of the corporation's existing 600 mortgages. The money will be re-invested in house-building and other schemes.

The front page of the first issue of the Milton Keynes Citizen, published on 1 October, 1981.

became an overnight success and went on to sweep all before it, despite one senior member of the Home Counties management team telling the Gazette staff at the time of its launch that it wouldn't last six months! Les Nunn, who was on the Gazette's advertising staff at the time, didn't believe him. The very next week he left the Gazette, joined the Citizen and recounts how selling advertising for the new newspaper to his old Gazette customers could not have been easier.

The Citizen began its life in Saxon Gate, Milton Keynes, where the YMCA now has its premises. Within a few months it had grown so fast that the operation needed bigger offices, found at Lloyds Court, in Central Milton Keynes. Keeping pace with the rapid growth of the city, its print run was now 75,000 and by 1987, with the pattern of growth continuing, it needed to move again, finding a new home at Linford Wood. It was at this time that Steve Larner, the Citizen's current news editor, joined the staff.

Steve recalls that three years on from there, in October 1990, the Citizen needed to move yet again as its overall expansion continued. The result was that what might now be called its permanent home was found when the offices were moved to new premises at Auckland Park, Bletchley. Ironically, they are only a stone's throw from the Gazette's old home in Ward Road, on the Mount Farm estate.

Attempts were made by the Citizen to open up similar newspapers in other areas, Steve remembers, but by then established newspapers were aware of the tactics and changed their own policies accordingly. It all boiled down to a game of strategies, Steve says, played by people who liked playing strategy games and trying to score points off each other. The end result, as far as the Citizen was concerned, was that it then concentrated its efforts purely on Milton Keynes, even to the extent of dropping off deliveries to the more far flung areas outside the city boundary. This meant it could keep up an effective balance between production costs and rising circulation within the city as more homes came on stream.

In 1987 Bill Alder and Gerry West sold out to East Midlands Allied

Press (EMAP) whilst staying with the company, but by the early 1990s they had moved on. EMAP consolidated the operation and by the middle of the decade a large chunk of EMAP's newspaper profits were generated by the Milton Keynes Citizen. However, more changes were to come and in 1996 EMAP sold off that part of their business covering regional newspapers to Johnston Press, based in Edinburgh. EMAP's jewel in the crown, the Milton Keynes Citizen, was part of the deal.

While the Citizen forged ahead, the established Milton Keynes newspapers suffered. The Bucks Standard sold out to become The Herald which in the fullness of time has also disappeared; the Wolverton Express and the Woburn Reporter, part of the old Westminster Press group, no longer exist and the Gazette also found life becoming more and more difficult as the 1980s progressed.

Things came to a head in the late autumn of 1985 when the Gazette's proprietors, Home Counties Newspapers, decided to close down the Ward Road premises. This led to a big row with the print and journalist unions and Trevor Johnson was involved as a negotiator on the union side. Things took an even uglier turn, Trevor tells me, when, in the midst of all the argy-bargy about jobs, a member of the proprietors' family turned up in Bletchley offering work because they were now taking over! The dispute took on a ring of nepotism, with Trevor appearing on Anglia television to say that the situation was grossly unfair. The editorial side wanted to keep going, and if the Gazette was up for sale, why had they not been informed as a staff, so that they might possibly orchestrate a local management buy-out?

Barclays Bank, it appears, were part-owners of the Gazette at the time and did not think much of the bad publicity. Trevor believes pressure was exerted somewhere, because the management buy-out then went ahead, with Trevor finding investors to keep the paper going. The actual title changed hands for only £10.

The Gazette was off the streets for only a week while Trevor and Gordon rushed around to advertisers and distributors alike to bring them upsides on the position. The editorial space at Ward Road was rented for a short time, before small offices were found in the Spring of 1986 in Aylesbury Street, Fenny Stratford, and for the first two years of its new life the Gazette held its own. But the recession of the late 1980s brought further problems, the paper struggled on into the 1990s but in 1993 it ceased publication.

All was not lost though for Trevor and Gordon, and a new company, Intermedia, was set up with Trevor as managing director. The enterprise now has offices in Bletchley Park and produces staff and specialist newspapers, in a high quality format, for a wide range of distinguished clients under the slogan 'Corporate communications which can really work'. The technology they use is very up to date, so I just wonder if the old adage of once bitten, twice shy, might occasionally flit through their minds... But Gordon still puts the day job behind him with his music, playing locally with Unit Six, the band he helped form more than 40 years ago and which, he believes, is now the oldest established band in the area.

A newer newspaper to appear recently is the MK News, which labels itself 'the independent voice of Milton Keynes'. With offices in the Brunel Centre in Bletchley, it is given away free but lacks the sheer bulk of the weekly package put out by the Citizen. Its reporting, however, is crisp and concise and, being the smaller package, its news stories are easy to find, not being lost in a welter of advertising. I wish it well. On the television front, both Anglia and BBC Look East give Milton Keynes adequate coverage, with Look East perhaps being slightly quicker off the mark. Anglia did have a regional office in Central Milton Keynes some ten years ago, but cut-backs dictated by head office in Norwich meant its closure.

From a news point of view all three journalists to whom I have spoken – Gordon, Trevor and Steve – agree that probably the two longest running items of reporting interest for Bletchley have been the decline of Queensway as a major shopping area and the role of Bletchley Park, both during its Second World War years and now as an international visitor attraction. Bletchley Park I will cover in a following

A selection of publications produced by Trevor Johnson and Gordon Hart under the 'Intermedia' label.

chapter and, having dealt with Queensway's decline earlier, let me now move on to plans to regenerate this area and, perhaps, Bletchley in general.

With Central Milton Keynes taking over as the commercial and civic centre of North Bucks in the mid-1980s, Wolverton found itself subject to many of the pressures being experienced by its more southerly neighbour, Bletchley. The Wolverton response, almost a decade later, was to hold a series of public meetings where it is true to say that many old adversaries buried the hatchet and decided to create a plan for the town's future based on genuine public interest. Milton Keynes Council, as the local authority, thought this a good idea and suggested that it could be the way forward for Bletchley. Accordingly, the Bletchley Partnership came into being and High Street names trading in the town, notably Boots and Sainsbury's, contributed money to fund the drawing up of a plan. A London company worked on the project and promised a hands-on approach, with the initial point of contact being an appointed town manager.

Stan Green, still conscious of his role as president of the Chamber of Trade, and John Mather, met with the consultants to discuss the plans but came away unimpressed. To Stan's way of thinking it seemed that what was being offered was regeneration to a standard format which had been used in other towns, and he argued that such an approach would not suit Bletchley because of its proximity to Central Milton Keynes. But as it was, nothing was to come of the overall scheme. Some aspects were achieved, such as the creation of the Bletchley Forum, an open discussion group, and the setting up of the Bletchley Business Association – shades, perhaps, of the old Chamber of Trade – of which Fenny Stratford businessman John Chapman became chairman. Former Milton Keynes councillor Robin Bowen-Williams, a stalwart of Bletchley rugger club, was elected as representative for the many bona-fide clubs in the town. Robin came to Bletchley in 1963 to teach at Bletchley Grammar School, where he was head of history and in 1973, when the Grammar merged with Wilton Secondary and became the Lord Grey school, Robin carried on his role at the new unit. He served on Milton Keynes Council from 1973–82.

However, interest in Bletchley's regeneration seemed to fade away, the town manager left, the Bletchley Forum lapsed and the Bletchley Partnership collapsed. It was not until the turn of the century that really positive plans began to appear when Milton Keynes Council brought the concept of neighbourhood councils into being. As a result of this, and following elections in 2001, Bletchley and Fenny Stratford Town Council emerged, as did West Bletchley Council.

Bruce Abbott, who lives in Vicarage Road, Fenny Stratford, was the headteacher of Bletchley's Leon School from 1981 until he retired in 1998. He served on the neighbourhood council which preceded the Bletchley and Fenny Stratford Council, to which he was elected, and the two new councils, alongside the Bletchley Business

Bruce Abbott, chairman of the Bletchley Development Board.

Association, Bletchley Forum, Milton Keynes Council and other interested parties, now work closely together under the banner of the Bletchley Development Board, which Bruce chairs, with Roger Bristow, from West Bletchley Council, as vice-chairman.

The Board's aim is to regenerate the town so that it will be regarded as a second centre for Milton Keynes, a move backed by Milton Keynes Council, and in the light of past disappointments, Bruce Abbott is upbeat and extremely optimistic about Bletchley's future.

It is a pretty pointless exercise, he thinks, to talk about Queensway reverting to what it was in the 1970s and Central Gardens being recreated. The 1970-style shops will never come back, he says, nor will the open space that was Central Gardens, and it is no use trying to 'patch-up' Bletchley.

There has to be radical change, he believes, and he hopes that in the next five years, the radical change will happen.

Among these major changes Bruce lists the proposed new professional football stadium at Denbigh, and the re-establishment of the east-west railway link between Cambridge and Oxford, as both having a big impact on Bletchley. What Bletchley has to do, he thinks, is to change to meet them and though he agrees that Queensway is still busy – national surveys have shown that the 'footfall' in Queensway, that is the number of people walking the thoroughfare, is high compared to other similar towns – he is not sure what people are buying there. Sainsbury's at one time, he recollects, was the most profitable Sainsbury's per till in the whole of the country, and the same was said of the Bejam frozen food centre which operated next door.

But that, of course, was before Central Milton Keynes took over with its concentration of national and international brand names which, coupled to the curiosity factor, pulled shoppers in from miles around. He agrees with me that Central Milton Keynes is now recognised, and indeed established, as a regional centre but feels there needs to be, for Milton Keynes people at least, another centre, and this could be Bletchley's role.

I asked if he and his fellow members of the Bletchley Development Board saw Queensway and the newer focal point of Bletchley shopping, the old Watling Street area, as remaining two separate enclaves of retailing and did they feel that the areas should be physically linked in some way.

His answer proved an interesting insight into the radical changes mentioned above. 'The Saxon Street Arcade', he said, meaning the idea of undercover retail outlets running from the Saxon Street–Princes Way

The Studio cinema, built in 1937, pictured when it closed in 1989 and, below, with its interior being gutted, is an example of Bruce Abbott's 'patchwork' regeneration of Bletchley. Modern offices now stand on the old cinema site.

roundabout back to the Watling Street, 'is a possibility in ten or twelve years time, and if the development takes off, it will take off quite rapidly and it will mushroom. But I think that does depend on the east-west rail link. If more houses are built to expand Milton Keynes to the west, then I think it even more important that Bletchley becomes a second centre. If people in these areas want a designer handbag, yes, they will continue to shop in Central Milton Keynes, but if they need groceries, or say a pair of shoes, then hopefully they would come into Bletchley. If any new development around Bletchley is quite considerable, then Bletchley has to seize its opportunity.'

This opportunity might have to manifest itself in demolishing large chunks of Queensway and rebuilding from scratch, he thinks, for there is little of architectural merit there at present – the remaining Victorian buildings seem not to be of a high quality and many of the shops are what he describes as 'horrible '50s–'60s style'.

Among other ideas being mooted, a summary of which was contained in the town council's newsletter 'The Neighbour' earlier this year, are a modification and/or expansion of the Leisure Centre so that it fronts on to Queensway by the old market site, and a closer look at the developments in and around the new college site close to the railway station and off Sherwood Drive. The newsletter noted the speculation about Bletchley Park's future with some of its grounds being used for housing, especially affordable housing for young families, and the future of the Stephenson House site which, in turn, could affect the bus station and the Brunel Centre, including the Sainsbury store.

What has surfaced from all the discussions on Bletchley's future is the positive need to make the town more welcoming from whichever direction it is entered. The original MKDC plans to loop Queensway with Saxon Street and Princes Way now look somewhat flawed for, if you are not familiar with the town layout, it is difficult to find your way into the shopping area of Queensway, as it is today. Entering from the west, for example, all you see as you drive under the railway bridge is a large roundabout apparently leading only back the way you have come

Bletchley's monstrosity, the multi-storey car park serving the Leisure Centre, comes down in 1999. Cars were often broken into or vandalised in the multi-storey which has given way to an open air parking lot.

and the black box of the Brunel Centre.

In 1967 Bletchley's town manager, John Smithie, told a meeting of the Bletchley Chamber of Trade that Bletchley must be a very important part of the new Milton Keynes and Bletchley station, he said, was the key to that importance. It is with this in mind that thoughts have been put forward to 'turn the station around' in the sense that the entrance would then face the Queensway area, not toward West Bletchley as it does now. I confess I see some merit in this as another part of the radical overhaul of the town, for in the past you could leave the station and from under the railway bridge the main thoroughfare stretched out before you. It doesn't now, as I have said above, and hasn't done since engineers constructed Saxon Street. But when that project was undertaken it was done with the best intentions in mind, that of linking Bletchley and Wolverton to the greenfield development of Milton

Keynes overall and giving the towns the importance of which John Smithie spoke in 1967. But as we all know now, the success of Central Milton Keynes threw that importance factor out of the window.

So, where do we go from here? Well, Bruce Abbott assured me that the former market site at the eastern end of Queensway, synonymous with its mushroom shaped coverings for stallholders which were burnt down in a fire a few years ago, will soon be redesigned and given a new name – favourites at the time of writing appear to be Elizabeth Square or Jubilee Square. The new design is looking to refurbish the paved area, create a small car park at the Prince's Way end, improve the lighting, build a covered entertainment area at the Cambridge Street end and brighten the place generally with appropriate seating and container planting.

In the longer term, Queensway might well become a pedestrian area closed to traffic and Bruce Abbott sees it as having a continental feel as a 'cafe society', particularly if Milton Keynes Council brings offices to Bletchley, where figures of 1000 staff have been mentioned. These council staff would want somewhere for a sandwich, light lunch or a pint of beer after work, he thinks, and along with trade from the day to day pedestrian traffic, he sees this as being the springboard for the continental-style cafe society. This kind of development, he feels, would also enhance Queensway out of office hours, for in his own words: 'If you walk down Queensway at half past six at night, it is just dead. There aren't even any bank robbers or hooligans about – they don't even go there!'

Another positive factor in the Development Board discussions is that any development should be co-ordinated, for the real danger is that piecemeal development would only add to the problems in the longer term. During this coming summer (2003) the Board means to re-launch the Bletchley Forum so that local opinions can be heard and to obtain premises in central Bletchley so that plans and ideas can be brought together in one place. This will allow residents to see for themselves what is being proposed and comment accordingly. In 35 years time, in

2038, I have no doubt Bletchley will want to celebrate the 200th anniversary of the coming of the railway. When it does, I wonder if the station entrance will face towards what is now Queensway instead of as it is today? And will premier division football be played by a team called Milton Keynes City at the Denbigh Stadium, clearly visible on one side from the trains that run between Oxford, Bedford and Cambridge, while on the other passengers get a good view of the Saxon Street arcade with its modern shops and offices? So many ifs and buts, maybe, but didn't we say exactly the same about Milton Keynes some 40 years ago? Change is ongoing; progress sometimes takes a little longer...

Bletchley, and some of the outlying areas such as Woburn Sands, did see both change and progress some ten years ago in relation to mains electricity supply, but for some reason it seemed hardly to be noticed.

With privatisation of the electricity supply industry having taken place, the supplier for our area, the East Midlands plc, found itself awash with money. Normal routine maintenance due at the time in many of the district's older streets – Western Road, Tavistock Street, Brooklands Road in Bletchley, for example, and in Woburn Sands Theydon Avenue and The Leys to name just two – meant the provision of new overhead cabling from the existing poles sunk into the ground. But someone, somewhere, decided there was enough money to upgrade and modernise the areas and so, almost overnight, the electricity poles disappeared and the new cabling was put underground. Ken Meadley, who is Bletchley born and bred and lives now in Highland Close, was a senior engineer with the company at the time and says it was almost uncanny how little comment was made by the local press or the people affected. Ken points out that it was, after all, a major engineering task.

But back to shopping just for a moment, for there are two areas of retail trading in Bletchley which have, I feel, provided a service, are well supported and contrast dramatically with the decline of Queensway. They are the Saturday market, pictured on these pages, and, collectively, the neighbourhood shopping areas such as Water Eaton, Melrose Avenue, Whaddon Way and others. The nearest to my home are the

Bletchley market, which has served the town well, in 1976 on its Albert Street site, with Bert Bates, complete with walking stick, who lived in Church Street. The bedraggled site on the Queensway area (opposite above), soon to be refurbished, after a fire destroyed the mushroom-shaped canopies in the early 1990s. And Margaret Dickman, (nee Lickorish) (opposite below) a Bletchley girl who grew up in Staple Hall Road, serves her customers on the present market site in Queensway. Margaret has been selling on the market since the early 1970s. She and her husband, John, live near Shefford, Beds.

Whaddon Way shops and Kiran and Gary Patel have worked hard over the years to make their 'Costcutter' operation there the true equivalent of the local 'corner shop'. They began with one unit in the early 1970s and often worked fourteen-hour days. But their hard work and enterprise paid off, in time they expanded, and now they occupy linked units which contain the local Past Office. In the early 1990s they won Asian Trader awards on a regular basis and their operation, and all the others in that precinct, are seen as friendly places to visit by a strong local customer base.

In spite of these local successes, however, the bottom line is that Queensway has lost out, as major shopping activity has swung a quarter of a mile to the east to premises on the Watling Street. Though these premises are not shops in the older term of the word, but more warehouses, they offer the public what they want and at reasonable prices. MFI, Matalan, Tesco, Wickes, Halfords and B&Q have all made their home in this area and look set to perform well for many years to

115

The start of real regeneration in Queensway? The Wilkinson store being built early in 2003 on the former Barclays Bank/Weatherburn Court site.

come. It is their presence and current success that might well be the launch pad for the development of a Saxon Street arcade.

Of course, the demise of Queensway and the general redevelopment of central Bletchley are not the only concerns of the town at present. The ongoing battle with Shanks regarding the future use of its infill site at neighbouring Newton Longville, which has been widely reported in the local press, and Bletchley's urgent need for a new cemetery, are particular concerns. Discussions are being held and much is going on to address both problems, so it is to be hoped that positive answers to these worries will be found sooner rather than later.

CHAPTER 6

CAREERING TOWARDS RETIREMENT

As I wrote in Chapter 1, the autumn of 1971 saw me working on the Beds and Bucks Observer at Leighton Buzzard. It was a comparatively easy task and as such I was keen to get back to London employment if something a little more senior and challenging came along. I scoured the trade newspapers and the quality dailies for several weeks and then, there it was. The Inner London Education Authority (ILEA), one of the biggest education authorities in the world, wanted an editor to set up and launch a house journal for its 48,000 strong academic staff.

I wrote off and was pleased to find that I was one of only three people short-listed for interview. I made the journey from my Bow Brickhill home to County Hall on London's South Bank for the appointment where, in some detail, the job was spelt out to me. It seemed that internal communication with such a large staff was a problem for the elected members of the Authority – under Labour control at the time – and its senior officers, headed by the education officer, Dr Eric Briault. The new magazine, to carry articles of topical interest for those employed in the teaching side of education, would make use of colour in its pages and be produced every week in term time.

I asked what I thought were some pertinent questions, such as the breakdown of staff in the various areas covered by the Authority, and the degree of control the chosen candidate would have in the design and production of the magazine.

The answer to my first question made me realise that, editorially, this would be a hard nut to crack if I got the job, for the readership would include the principals and senior lecturers in the five polytechnics controlled by the Authority, right through the standard educational pattern of secondary and primary schools, the latter to include young teachers fresh from training school and undertaking what was known as their first London appointments – FLAs. On top of that there were all those people teaching in the further education colleges, adult education institutes and special schools. Now this was a bit like asking the same man to edit the Daily Telegraph, Hello magazine, the Sun and the Racing Post, so wide did I recognise the personal levels of readership to be! And on the production side, it seemed I had asked a sticky question, for the idea was to hand over the design and production of the magazine to the Greater London Council's (GLC) reprographics department, the GLC being the co-occupier of County Hall. When I queried who had the ultimate say over the design and use of illustration in the magazine, and intimated that it had to be the editor because it was he who held sole legal responsibility, I felt that some of my interviewing panel were getting a bit prickly.

Wading into even deeper water – as I was to learn later – I pointed out forcibly that in addition to this area of responsibility, the editor should have total control over the magazine's content, though common sense, I said, meant he should seek advice. In short, there should be no censorship by the senior officers or politicians, because if there was, then the journal would soon be seen at worst as a sop to the teaching unions and at best, little more than a public relations exercise by the Authority.

I reckoned I had nothing to lose by being up-front and, as I thought, totally professional about how the exercise should be mounted, for I confess it was the sort of professionalism that I had learned and put into practice at Marshall Cavendish. But I got it wrong – or so I thought – for after some deliberating by the interview board, with me sitting in an ante-room, I was told 'thanks, but no thanks.' So, somewhat disappointed, for I would have loved the challenge, I travelled back to

Bow Brickhill and the deputy editor's job on the Beds and Bucks Observer at Leighton Buzzard.

It was on my half-day off the next week and while playing golf on the Leighton course, that the clubhouse got a message to me. My wife had been on the 'phone telling me to get home quickly and get in touch with the ILEA that same afternoon. Well, I did as 'The Management', as I call her, wanted, and when I arrived back at Bow Brickhill, Barbara said she was convinced they had changed their mind and were going to offer me the job. I didn't think they were, but thought that I might be in line for the deputy editor's post, which was to be part of the proposed editorial team. Again, I got it wrong and 'The Management' was right. It seemed the fellow who was offered the job changed his mind soon after it was put before him and the ILEA decided to take a chance on me. I joined the ILEA staff a few weeks before Christmas.

I spent the first couple of weeks in intense talks with a Mrs Ena Chaplin, who had been on the interviewing board and who had political responsibility for that area of the ILEA's work, and several senior officers, including Dr Briault. I stuck to my guns and found I had a staunch ally in no less a person than the Leader of the Authority himself, Ashley Bramall, later to become Sir Ashley Bramall. I was given a completely free hand across all areas of the proposed magazine and in return I gave an undertaking not to be afraid to ask for advice. I moved into a sizeable open plan office on the ground floor of County Hall, given a senior clerical officer to handle the administration and a junior clerk to carry out telephone reception and basic office duties, and told, in effect: 'O.K. Now go and recruit your staff and tell the graphic designers of the GLC what you want them to do.' I was like the proverbial dog with two tails and it was to be the beginning of a 16 year stay with the Authority. The first eight years were extremely self-satisfying; the second eight years were not quite so enjoyable.

Dick Davison, the 26-year-old education correspondent of Newcastle's evening newspaper, became my deputy editor, with Pam Hill, the deputy head of one of ILEA's primary schools on board to keep us in touch with classroom affairs and handle the review columns for books and other educational materials. The contingent from the GLC was headed by Reg Corke, so well qualified in design and print matters that it wasn't true, and Reg was aided and abetted by three designers and a clerical assistant. I made sure they moved in with me.

We launched the magazine on the Queen's birthday in April 1972 and called it 'ILEA Contact'. Although there was some reader hostility from some quarters, by and large it was hailed a success. Within six months that initial hostility had gone, teachers were clamouring to use the magazine as an effective means of communication with the Authority, and we took our first national award. Between 1972 and 1980, when the format of the journal was changed from its A4 colour magazine style, we took 17 national and international awards. It was a very, very satisfying period in my career and with it came promotion to managing editor of all ILEA publications, some 120 titles in all. There were also some wonderful personal spin-offs from 'Contact's success, not least a fulfilled ambition with a trip to the United States where, alongside my formal lecturing tasks, my interest in the culture and history of the Native American brought an unexpected reward.

My interest in Native Americans began in the late 1950s when Barbara and I went to the Studio cinema in Bletchley to see Errol Flynn in a film called 'They died with their boots on.' It was typical Hollywood goodies and baddies and Flynn played the part of Colonel George Armstrong Custer, commander of the 7th cavalry who was killed fighting the combined Sioux and Cheyenne bands at the Little Big Horn river in June, 1876. A couple of weeks after seeing the film I found a book entitled 'Death on the Prairie', written by a man named Paul Wellman. The book told the story of the various Plains Indian wars and recounted in some detail the Little Big Horn fight. Chalk and cheese would be an apt description of the Hollywood version and the hard facts, as they were known then. Since then archaeological discoveries at the site of the Little Big Horn battle have proved quite conclusively that there was no 'last stand' by Custer and his men, as history would previously have led us to believe, and that the 7th cavalry were routed by an enemy who were better armed – they had repeating rifles, the cavalry had single-shot breach loaders – and whose battlefield tactics were superior. In addition, we now know that the troops that Custer had under his command were not seasoned veterans, again as history would have us believe, but a rag-tag bag of misfits and barely trained men who had never seen combat. Last year (2002) Channel 4 television presented an excellent programme telling the real story based on the new evidence.

All those years ago, however, the fact that a top American general was 'out-cavalried' by so called 'savages' sent me off on a quest whereby I devoured every piece of written material I could find on the Plains Indians, of whom the combined bands and tribes of the Sioux were the most feared and powerful. In time my research led me to the tribes of the far south, such as the Seminole, Choctaw and Cherokee, to those north of the Canadian border, the Iroquois, Huron, Delaware and Mohawk, and finally to my major area of study, the Apache nation of the south-west, the very last major tribal gathering to be subjugated by the white man.

I soon discovered that in the mid-1800s the Chiricahua Apache, though one of the smallest groups of the nation, was looked upon as the heart of its society, due in no small measure to the stature of its warrior but very statesmanlike leader, Cochise. The book 'Blood Brother', by Elliot Arnold, tells the story of Cochise's friendship with a U.S. Army scout, Tom Jeffords, and how Cochise was instrumental in bringing peace between the whites and the Apaches. In reading this you will no doubt realise by now that I could go on and on. But let me stop this part of my tale by saying that I wrote to the remnants of Cochise's Chiricahua band in the 1960s and as a result was allowed to take the tribal name of Pionsenay, which means horse. I chose this because it was Crazy Horse, of the Sioux, who defeated Custer at the Little Big Horn, and that historical fact set me off on what is an ongoing interest in matters Native American. If you want just one book on the subject, then read

The monument to the 19th century Nez Perce war in Idaho, U.S.A.

'Bury my heart at Wounded Knee', by Dee Brown. I guarantee it will give you a new slant on the 'democratic' America of the time.

In 1974 I took a telephone call in my County Hall office from the Cultural Affairs office of the American Embassy in Grosvenor Square. I knew the staff there quite well and I was asked if I could arrange a programme of talks to London schools by a Nez Perce descendant of a famous chief of that tribe, Chief Lawyer. I said I could, the programme was arranged, and I then met up with David Rogers, the young man in question and some years my junior, who is the great-grandson of Chief Lawyer. I knew that the Nez Perce homelands were the plateau areas of what we now know as Idaho and Oregon, and David and I got on like a house on fire. Two years later, in 1976, I spent three weeks with him while lecturing, visited his friends and family, and was made very welcome by whites and Native Americans alike. David's aunt and tribal elder, Mylie Lawyer, who spent many years working with the United States Bureau of Indian Affairs, gave me an excellent dinner one evening,

The author, looking somewhat out of place in an English business suit, sitting atop an old western stage coach in Oregon in 1976.

Nez Perce tepees used by holiday makers in modern day Idaho.

123

Just like a scene from Hollywood – rugged Oregon countryside captured on camera in 1976.

in which I was introduced to traditional Nez Perce fare. And after the meal she had a gift for me, a beautiful beaded medallion which she had made herself. As she slipped it over my head, she told me that I was now her English nephew and I was part of the family. From that day on David and I have referred to each other as big and little brother!

There was one other major surprise in store on that trip. David's job was that of a deputy sheriff for Umatilla County, Oregon, and after spending some time in the company of his boss, the County sheriff, Bill McPherson, I was taken on to the staff as an honorary deputy. I was given formal identification papers, voice-printed, finger-printed, given a uniform, taken to the armoury and chose a handgun, had some practice on the police shooting range and then rode with David on several night patrols where I will only say here that proper police work was entered into! I still have the uniform today – but I had to leave the .357 Colt Python magnum handgun behind!

When Mrs Thatcher became Britain's first woman premier in 1979, it was clear that she would tighten the screw on educational spending, following her years as the Conservative minister for education. By the next year, 1980, budgets throughout the ILEA were pruned drastically and one of the casualties was 'Contact' in its magazine form. It was decided that it should be produced in tabloid newspaper format and, luckily for me, that didn't pose any problems, so I held on to my job. It did mean, though, the end of an eight years association with Reg Corke and the GLC designers, and I can tell you it was quite a goodbye party! Reg lives in East Peckham, in Kent, by chance the village where I learned to walk in a cherry orchard as a baby, where my parents and grandparents used to go hop-picking and where, in 1940 as a six-years-old, I saw a Spitfire bring down a German 'plane during the Battle of Britain.

There were other changes afoot in County Hall in the early 1980s, for Sir Ashley Bramall was deposed as Leader of the Labour group and an Islington left-winger, Frances Morrell, took over. Suddenly, everything had to be ultra-politically correct and it became clear to me that the emphasis of what County Hall was about had changed. When I joined the Authority in 1971 I felt that the administration used the building as its headquarters for educating children first and as a power base for its politics, second. Under Mrs Morrell I couldn't help but think that things were reversed. The morale of the whole place just seemed to plummet and was made even worse when, in the mid-1980s, Mrs Thatcher decided to abolish the Greater London Council, the Authority with whom we shared County Hall and whose Leader was a well-known left wing figure, Ken Livingstone, currently the Mayor of London. Suddenly there were departmental and staff re-organisations and many former GLC staff were taken on by the ILEA. Many of them, I have to say, had little or no idea what their new job was all about. What was apparent was that they were being 'saved' because of their political persuasions.

By now I was becoming very disillusioned and it didn't need a brilliant brain to realise that Mrs Thatcher only had to lower the sights of her cannon a degree or two to blow the ILEA out of the water, as she had done with the GLC. As the uncertainties about the future of the ILEA grew in 1985, Barbara and I made the decision to move from Bow Brickhill.

In 1982 my father had died and within two years my mother, who had suffered a series of strokes from 1978 onwards, had also passed away. After Dad died, mother became a resident at The Cedars, a Beds County Council home at Ampthill and from where, most weekends, we would bring her to Bow Brickhill. As a result of this we had extended the house in 1982 so that she had her own large bedroom, complete with en-suite facilities, and at the same time we added to our own living accommodation. 'Tub' Carruthers, a village builder, and his partner, Graham Whitmee, from Woburn Sands, built the extension. However, within three weeks in the summer of 1984 we attended two funerals and a wedding. Barbara's cousin, Don Gilks, who was born and bred in Bow Brickhill, died at the early age of 53, mother died, and our son, Mark, was married and set up home with his wife at Newport Pagnell. This meant that there were now only the three of us, myself, Barbara and our daughter, Rachel, rattling around in a rather large house. The upshot of our decision to move came to fruition in October 1985 when we moved into our present home in Elmers Park, Old Bletchley. Some 18 years on, it is a move we have never regretted, although our initial intention was to move to Woburn Sands.

By the time we had settled into our new Bletchley home I had decided to get out of the ILEA before Mrs Thatcher fired the shots which would send the Authority into the same oblivion afforded the GLC. And by the end of the decade, she had taken the necessary action.

I found what seemed to be the right sort of job at the end of 1986. The British Dental Association (BDA) wanted a director to set up a new department of communications and public affairs, and I joined the Association at its Wimpole Street offices in west London early the following year.

I found the BDA a somewhat archaic institution. Although the body's ruling council realised the need for a more open administration whereby the public could have direct access to a representative, and the whole ethos of the BDA needed to be more user friendly and customer orientated, I soon found that what was wanted and what, in fact, I was going to be allowed to do to achieve those goals, were poles apart. Early on I remember giving my opinion on how we should word a press release that was to go out, where the salient point for any Fleet Street journalist was the amount of monies involved. But some of my fellow directors – there were six of us – who had been with the BDA for many years, wanted the main thrust of the story to be its aspects of dental care. When I had the temerity to query why they felt this way, they gave me the oldest excuse in the world. 'Well, we've never done it like this before . . .'

Though I like to think I did achieve some major breakthroughs, particularly in relation to internal communication whereby the practising dentist was told more about what was going on within the association, it became increasingly clear as the months went on that I was getting nowhere.

Although I was being employed to do a professional communicator's job, I wasn't being allowed to communicate. Instead, the Association seemed more concerned as to how many toothpaste companies could I sign up to advertise in its own literature or to sponsor the Association for something or other. It seemed its definition of communications and public affairs was a little different from mine and neither of us knew that until we were both committed. By late 1988 the Association and I agreed to differ once too often, and parted company.

At the age of 54 it's not often that a job you have always hankered after, however successful or unsuccessful you may have been, actually comes your way. But that, I am very pleased to say, was exactly what happened to me at this stage in my career.

Commuting to London was getting worse. The trains seemed more crowded, the rolling stock that replaced older type carriages didn't seem so comfortable, punctuality was slipping, and the trains never seemed clean. On top of all that, the fares were going up and up. When

I began commuting in 1969, I could travel from Bletchley right through to Leicester Square on the underground for the princely sum of £100 a year. By 1988, I was looking at more than £2000 a year, and that's after tax, of course, to do the same thing. I shudder to think what the cost must be now.

But fortune smiled on me again; there would be no more commuting, for, following my mentor Carl Moser nearly 20 years earlier, I joined Milton Keynes Development Corporation to handle its media affairs. It was the job I'd often thought about and now I left home at 8.15 am and was behind my desk only ten minutes later. In the summer of 1989 I could mow the lawn after work, any day of the week, not just at weekends. I suddenly realised how much time I had spent sitting on trains just to get to work and I relished promoting Milton Keynes via the media and, over a period of time, working on aspects of marketing events and ceremonial occasions. I was to be with the Development Corporation until it was wound up by the then Secretary of State for the Environment, Michael Heseltine, on 31 March 1992. The three and a bit years with the Corporation gave me even more job satisfaction than had those early years with the Inner London Education Authority.

One of the first tasks to come my way with MKDC was to organise a photo shoot for the Daily Telegraph to show the world that Britain's newest town could grow willow trees and turn them into cricket bats! I enlisted the help of former Bletchley Town cricketer Tony Clarke, an old friend from my junior reporter days on the Gazette when he, and his father, Jim, used to play football together for Bletchley Boys Brigade Old Boys. Padded up and in his whites, I had Tony shaping up to play in a stand of bat-willow trees by the river alongside the Haversham railway viaduct.

The three or more years seemed to go very quickly with, seemingly, a special flurry of activity towards the end. In early October 1991, for example, I liaised with former Milton Keynes mayor Councillor Roger Bristow in a project whereby Milton Keynes engineering apprentices built a replica of the famous 'Bloomer' locomotive once built at

Deputy sheriff Ted Enever 'frisks' MKDC general manager Frank Henshaw on Comic Relief day 1992 outside the Corporation's Saxon Court headquarters. All public parking in Milton Keynes was then free; money for comic relief was raised by charging MKDC staff to park.

Wolverton works. The 'Bloomer' was the Victorian railway equivalent of Concorde, for nothing before could compare with its speed, grace and power. When the loco was built, with, I am told, the name of each apprentice on the inner side of an individual rivet, schools were invited to the unveiling outside Central Milton Keynes railway station.

I booked Jon Pertwee, in the role of his Dr Who character, to appear for the unveiling, scripting the event so that Roger, Jon Pertwee and myself all appeared as Victorian characters lost in a time warp that had transported us to modern Milton Keynes. Roger was a schoolmaster, Jon was of course Dr Who, arriving in the station forecourt by stagecoach, and I was the stationmaster who had to meet them both. The three of us interacted with the hundreds of children there who loved every minute of it – as did we – even though it poured with rain and everybody got soaked. Most importantly, from the professional standpoint, we made national television and radio. And the 'Bloomer' stands just as proudly outside the station today as it did when it was unveiled by Jon Pertwee twelve years ago.

The final accolade in the Corporation's history was the visit of the Queen just before being closed down in 1992. I wrote of her visit in 'Changing Faces, Changing Places' and it really was a most memorable day. Just after that visit MKDC held a special evening when all former staff were invited to the Saxon Court headquarters for a farewell drink and a chat. I felt particularly proud that evening when, as my special guest, I took along Carl Moser, for as events were to show, it was the last time we were to spend any length of time in each other's company, for he died suddenly later that year.

On Tuesday, 31 March we were paid off and I officially took early retirement at the age of 57. It took a full 48 hours before the enormity of that decision sunk in and close on four years before I could really convince myself that my time was my own. But was it? I've never been the sort of fellow who could sit around watching television all day or generally doing nothing. I like to keep myself busy and keep occupied.

So, even before that last day with the Corporation arrived, I found myself making commitments in relation to the battle to save from the developers' bulldozers Bletchley's Second World War code-breaking centre, Bletchley Park.

CHAPTER 7

BLETCHLEY PARK

The place we know now as the hub of Allied codebreaking activity during the Second World War, Bletchley Park has always held a special place in the affections of local people. This stems from the days when Bletchley Park was the home of financier Sir Herbert Leon who, with his wife, Lady Fanny, did much to benefit Bletchley, Fenny Stratford and the local population at large. The Leons have left their mark in many ways, and just two that spring to mind are the naming of the Leon recreation ground on the Bletchley–Fenny borders and the Leon School. All in all, the Leons were the epitome of Victorian employers and were highly regarded by their staff and townspeople alike.

After Sir Herbert died in 1926, Lady Fanny continued with the running of the estate until her death in January 1937, when the Bletchley District Gazette reported:'Lady Leon can, without dispute, be described as Bletchley's greatest benefactress. Her generosity towards and interest in many of the town's organisations are well known. What will never be fully known are those many acts of kindness which have so endeared her to the people of Bletchley.'

The Leons' son, George, had made his own way in life, did not want to take on the mantle of responsibility for the estate, which included tracts of land over and above what we know as the Park today, and decided to dispose of everything, which was split into various lots and duly sold off. One such lot was Bletchley Park as it is now, that is the area bounded by Sherwood Drive, Whalley Drive and Church Green Road, and this was bought by Captain Hubert Faulkner, a local entrepreneur whose plan was to demolish The Mansion, the Leon family's home, build himself a new house slightly to the south by the lake, and use other areas for residential development.

Though some property in the stable yard was taken down, the remainder was left untouched for, in the following year, 1938, agents representing a branch of the Government's Foreign Office, the Government Code and Cypher School (GC&CS) made an approach to Captain Faulkner. The School, it seemed, was looking for a quiet country home from which to carry out its duties. GC&CS took a short lease on the Park under the perhaps bizarre name of 'Captain Ridley's shooting party' but were soon back as its new owners.

From then on the rest is history, as they say. From some 200 staff in 1938 the Park grew to employ some 7000 people in 1944 when Allied forces invaded Hitler's occupied Europe and so ensured victory. Some will say as many as 12000 worked in the Park during these wartime years, but I prefer to accept the figure of 7000 given to me by no less a person than the late Sir Harry Hinsley, the Government's official wartime historian and who worked as a codebreaker in the Park from its earliest days until the end of the war in 1945, when he was its deputy director.

What is not in dispute is that Bletchley Park's codebreaking work, and its development of the world's first electronic, programmable computer, 'Colossus' in 1943, shortened the Second World War by at least two years and so saved thousands of lives on both sides. But in the peace that followed six years of conflict, Bletchley Park guarded its secrets well. Having signed the Official Secrets Act before joining the Park's staff, the codebreakers were very reluctant to talk about their wartime work and its great importance. It was not until the 1970s that the world at large had some inkling of the magnificent task that was carried out there between 1938–45. It was then clear that Bletchley Park was a site of national importance.

After victory in 1945 the codebreakers left and Bletchley Park was taken over jointly by central Government and the Post Office, the forerunner of British Telecom. Within the complex, post office engineers of a variety of grades and disciplines were trained, and on the Government side the Civil Aviation Authority also established training facilities there for many years, finally departing in the early-1990s.

Somewhat earlier than this, in 1986, Milton Keynes Development Corporation and Milton Keynes Borough Council jointly adopted 'A plan for Bletchley' which, though non-statutory, did go through public participation and conformed with the Bucks County Structure Plan. The policy of this plan stated clearly that 'Bletchley Park be allocated as a "special study" area in which favourable consideration might be given to some high technology, science based, office/industrial development, training/educational, institutional and possibly some residential development, subject to the preparation of a master plan for the development of the area which has been approved by the planning authorities.'

As things moved on, Milton Keynes Borough Council's Planning Committee resolved in December 1989 that a development brief should be prepared for the Park which allowed for a higher level of residential development than indicated in earlier plans. In addition, the Planning Committee also considered, on 10 January 1990, the possible development of land adjacent to the Park on its extreme north-east boundary and known as 'the playing field'. All the ideas emerged as an entity in a development brief for the Park which was made public in May 1990. It was clear from this that the Park could soon become a residential site accommodating up to 200 houses.

The following year, 1991, Bletchley was full of rumour and counter rumour as to the fate of what local people called 'our wooden huts' – a reference to the earliest wartime buildings which could be clearly seen by anyone passing the Park gates in Wilton Avenue and which were assumed to be the area where housing would go. What many did not realise at the time was the scale of brick and concrete buildings that lay behind the huts, out of site and extending towards Sherwood Drive, and that this was where the bulk of housing might go.

By the summer of 1991 the Bletchley Archaeological and Historical Society (BAHS), with Little Brickhill's Ena Halmos as chairperson, began to worry that the wartime history of the Park would be lost forever if developers moved in. As a result, the Society began to formulate plans for a reunion of codebreakers and support staff for October of that year, the object being to document as much historical fact about the wartime operations as possible. As plans began to take positive shape, the date given for the reunion was Saturday 19 October, some 50 years to the day since a letter was sent direct to prime minister Winston Churchill, by Alan Turing and other senior staff at the Park, requesting more resources. Churchill's response to the letter was to tell his aide, General Ismay: 'Action this day!'

That Saturday was a day I will never forget, for it marked the beginning of my own association with Bletchley Park. As I have written earlier, only a short time before the Park reunion I worked closely with former Milton Keynes mayor, Councillor Roger Bristow, on the 'Bloomer' locomotive project for the station forecourt area of Central Milton Keynes. About a week before the planned gathering, Roger asked what did I know about Bletchley Park's history and I told him very little, other than that it was a wartime codebreaking centre and the first computer was invented there. It was off the back of this that he then asked if I would go along to give both codebreakers and Archaeological and Historical Society members – of which he was one – some advice as to how the threat to the Park could be given a national profile. We discussed various options and by the time I stood before some 200 very distinguished people to say my piece, I was able to recommend a letter direct to the current prime minister, John Major, so emulating the 1941 letter to Churchill, a media campaign involving letters to Fleet Street newspapers and, with hindsight, possibly the most ambitious undertaking of all, the formation of a charitable Trust to harness public opinion.

The codebreakers listened to me very attentively and at the end of my address came up with some very positive thoughts. The first was

A group of visitors assemble for a tour of Bletchley Park earlier this year; the tours were begun by Bletchley Park Trust volunteers in February, 1994.

that 'the young man' – I was 57 – being a journalist, should compose the letter to the prime minister, which the most senior of their members could then sign on the spot; the second that a Trust was a good idea but that would probably have more impact if it were Bletchley based. The result of this was that what I thought was going to be a quick chat and then home turned into a full afternoon suddenly immersed in the most fascinating of subjects. As far as Bletchley Park was concerned, I was hooked.

I duly composed and ran off the letter to prime minister John Major on a word processor and it was signed by several of the dignitaries there. I delivered it to Downing Street the following Monday, when en route to a business meeting in London.

With regard to the formation of a Trust, Dr Peter Jarvis, another BAHS member whom I had known for many years for he was my family's general practitioner, kindly offered the use of his Church Green

Road home for a meeting, and several people said they would be interested in attending. Among them was Tony Sale, a computer expert who was secretary of the Computer Conservation Society and working at that time as a senior curator at the Science Museum, Peter Wescombe, who had done much to organise the reunion, and Ena Halmos. Within two weeks, in early November, we met at the Jarvis's home with Peter's wife, Sue, being good enough to take minutes and Tony Sale's wife, Margaret, also prepared to help in any way she could. The meeting asked me to act as chairman, with Roger Bristow as vice-chairman, and by the end of an enthusiastic evening we had the basic structure of a charitable Trust down on paper. I talked to my planning colleagues at Milton Keynes Development Corporation the next day and they were happy to use the Steering Committee, as we had called ourselves, as a consultant group to produce a video and historical brief relating to the Trust's possible aims and objectives. As a committee we put the brief together in a very short space of time and asked Mark Dyson, the local Anglia television correspondent, to help us out with the video. This he did, in his own time, and the end product was a first rate job.

In early February, 1992, Milton Keynes Borough Council did Bletchley an enormous favour by declaring most of Bletchley Park a conservation area and, three days later, on 11 February, the Bletchley Park Trust was born. What lay before the Trust was a long and arduous campaign, but it was ready for the fight.

The Steering Committee had put together a Board of Trustees which was headed by Professor Peter Thewlis, then principal of De Montfort's Milton Keynes Polytechnic, later to become De Montfort University. As his vice-chairman was Sir Philip Duncombe, who I had known for many years and who, in truth, I had asked to be chairman, but pressure of other commitments meant he could not take it on. Peter and Sue Jarvis became Trustees, as did local businessmen John Discombe, Ken King, John Mather, John Williams and John Napleton, a director at the Development Corporation, among several others. Meetings were held

A Second World War night in 1993 in Hut 8, Bletchley Park, then the Post Office social club, in aid of funds for the Bletchley Park Trust. Pictured are, left to right: Rachel Enever, Barbara Enever, James Bristow, Ted Enever, Peter Thewlis, the Trust chairman. Hut 8 is now a visitors' restaurant.

in one of the Civil Aviation Authority rooms in 'A' block on the Park.

Day to day activities centred on Roger Bristow's office in Denbigh House, from where he ran his own small marketing and promotions company. When I took early retirement on the wind-up of the Development Corporation the following month, March, the Trustees asked me to act as chief executive, to which I agreed, with Roger as general manager and Tony Sale giving us what time he could spare as a technical consultant.

That first year seemed to fly by as the workload grew and we continued to pressure both Government and British Telecom to give us favourable terms to buy the Park outright. But the figures they were coming up with were running into millions and there was no way we had access to that kind of money.

Still, we kept beavering away, though by the beginning of 1993 it was clear we were in for a very long haul and finances were tight, to say the least. Around this time John Mather's good offices found us a new home in Queensway, close to Westfield Road – the building is now the Veggie World cafe and take-away. The accommodation meant Roger, Tony and I could operate from the first floor, while on the ground floor local volunteer helpers in the form of Vic Hamilton, June Claisse-Carter, Ray Dawson, Richard Minney and Martin Baggott, assisted by others, set up an exhibition featuring the Park's wartime role and other Second World War memorabilia.

Roger was very busy at this time talking to Bob Watson, who lives in Rickley Lane, and with his help, measuring in detail and getting down on paper as much historical information as he could on all the individual wartime buildings in the Park. Bob's family had worked in the service of the Park for many years and Bob was in the thick of the rushed building work of the wooden huts at the outbreak of war. Tony was beginning to formulate plans for the building of a working replica of 'Colossus' while, for my part, I kept up the marketing and public relations side with a steady flow of news stories to the press, coupled with various fund raising activities.

One of these was the biggest dance Bletchley had ever seen and held at the Leisure Centre. Some 800 people, most in 1940s dress, danced to the music of the Opus One band, a Glen Miller-style orchestra backed by the famous Beverley Sisters, who were themselves discovered by Miller when they were evacuees in Northampton during the war years. It was he who persuaded the BBC to give them a contract and they sang their way into the hearts of Britain over the years. They and Opus One certainly did us proud that night in a Leisure Centre decorated as if it was the height of the London Blitz in 1940. We even managed to have a barrage balloon hanging from the roof! Such was the success of the evening that we repeated it the next year with a D-Day theme to commemorate the 50th anniversary of the Normandy landings in 1944.

The Opus One big band pose for a publicity shot in front of a Second World War Dakota aircraft.

By now we were confident we had the whole of Bletchley behind us as more and more people came forward to get involved. When we learned that British Telecom had invited the Secretary of State for the Environment, Michael Howard, to Bletchley so that we could give him a tour of the Park and explain our objectives, we felt we were getting somewhere.

Michael Howard came to Bletchley in May 1993 and after a presentation at De Montfort University he was given a lightning tour of the Park by David Hartley, who was acting as Trust architect. At the end of it all the minister paid us a wonderful compliment. 'You have achieved a great deal with limited resources,' he said, 'but it is now clear you need some extra help. I am now going away to get you that help.'

The help came in the form of an independent feasibility study undertaken by Coopers and Lybrand and by the late summer of 1993 the study upheld the Trust's arguments over the past two years that a museum, conference and educational/training complex could be set up in the Park's Mansion and refurbished wartime buildings.

Meetings with the relevant Government department and British Telecom continued, but now on a better footing, and in December 1993 the Trust was given permission to use certain buildings on the Park so as to make a start on its museum provision. Roger, Tony and I, with Roger's wife Ruth running the general office as she had done from day one, promptly moved on to the Park and set up our headquarters in the bungalow building in the stable yard. The building was used in the Leon's time as an apple, pear and plum store. By February of 1994 we were opening to the public and, with the help of Peter and Sue Jarvis and others, began to give guided tours of the area, pointing out the wartime usage of most of the buildings.

By June, we were able to offer visitors the added attractions of a superb collection of Churchill memorabilia owned by Jack Darrah and his wife, a Luton couple, an exhibition of materials salvaged from crashed 'plane sites by the Buckinghamshire Aircraft Recovery Group, formed in 1991 by Martin Baggot and his associates, and displays on the lake by the Leighton Buzzard Model Boat Club.

Though still carrying out the nominal duties of Trust chief executive, restructuring meant that Tony Sale and I were by now both Trustees with Roger Bristow acting as general manager. In the early months of 1994 we were approached by Sutton Publishing to produce a guide book for the Park which at that time we felt unable to do. But off the back of this approach we did formulate the idea of a guide-cum-historical record-cum Trust story which, Sutton said, they would need quickly. The result was that the Board of Trustees gave me permission to enter into a personal contract with Sutton to produce such a book and, in return, I offered to donate my royalties to the Trust on any direct sales of the publication it might make. The end result was that I wrote 'Britain's Best Kept Secret – Ultra's base at Bletchley Park' in three weeks flat, complete with many photographs and illustrations. I expected the book to have a shelf life of about two years, but it is still selling now. As a result of its success, the Trust accorded me the privilege some three years ago of becoming a patron.

In the summer of 1994 a family bereavement meant a rearranged holiday and this in turn led to me missing the visit of H.R.H the Duke of Kent to Bletchley Park. When I returned I noticed a distinct cooling of amiability on the part of some of my Board colleagues and other Trust associates. I was surprised further when Sutton publishing reported to me that they had received a letter complaining of the personal contract the company had entered into with me and demanding that 'Britain's Best Kept Secret' be reclassified as a Trust book.

I have no intention of naming the writer of that letter here, but Sutton made it clear to the person concerned that the book was mine and, by the terms of my contract with the company, the Trust stood to benefit. I asked the chairman, Peter Thewlis, to reiterate at the next Board meeting that I had the Board's permission to enter into contract with Sutton.

At the next meeting shall we just say I was not surprised that the meeting ended, having 'run out of time' as it was put, before my item on the agenda was reached. I was appalled at what I regarded as very unprofessional behaviour concerning the whole incident and resigned as a Trustee shortly afterwards. However, I continued to support the Trust informally by giving talks, continuing to assist the media on Park matters and, where possible, fund raising. I had no formal contact with the Trust until 1999 when Sir Philip Duncombe, by then chairman of a new Board and restructured administration, was able to assist me on an update of 'Britain's Best Kept Secret'.

That update told of the expansion of the Trust's initial exhibition in the Park and the basis of the current cryptology trail, explaining the breaking of the Enigma codes in detail. It also covered another visit of the Duke of Kent, on 6 June 1996, the 52nd anniversary of D-Day, when, as chief patron, he came to switch on a working replica of Colossus. Tony Sale's dream had become a reality, but only after Tony and a dedicated team of helpers had spent many, many hours of painstaking technical work. Dr Tom Flowers, who in 1943 was the original designer of Colossus, was also on hand to see the switch-on but, sadly, died two years later in 1998.

In March of that year Christine Large, the current Park director – the term chief executive was dropped – was appointed and headed negotiations with British Telecom and Government involving a four strand approach to running the Park. They were:

The Heritage Zone, to encompass the main museum, to show how the Park worked in wartime and to look into modern communications technology;

The Conference Zone, which would comprise a media centre and aim to attract academic users;

The Community Zone, where educational and social facilities would be provided for both volunteers and local people, with a company that would train and employ disabled citizens;

The Knowledge Zone, an area designed to appeal to the knowledge industries.

With these four zones the Trust aimed to create a heritage park with the overall theme being 'The Science of Communications'. Alongside this mainstream activity mention must be made of the many support groups working with the Trust and which form additional visitor attractions. In 1999, when a large chunk of the Park's acreage was finally handed to the Trust, more than two dozen groups called Bletchley Park home.

Further re-organisation of the Trust at the turn of the century saw many of the Board of Trustees put in a position of having to resign, Sir Christopher Chataway taking over from Sir Philip Duncombe as chairman, though Sir Philip is still involved, and administrative staff are

A target of the media rather than targeting the media. Ted Enever puts the Bletchley Park case to a television reporter outside 10 Downing Street in 1993.

increasing considerably. Though I know the change of chairmanship was amiable enough, I think that some of the other changes have caused tension between the Trust and the support groups. I would hope that in the foreseeable future any differences might quickly be sorted out, one of the underlying causes being, I suspect, that paid Trust staff are finding themselves being placed in positions whereby they need to tell volunteers – many of whom have given the Trust freely of their time and expertise over the years – what they can and cannot do. If this is this case, and it may well be a very big if, it might just be a breakdown of communication which I hope might be readily resolved. As the voluntary groups need the Trust to give them a home, so equally, the Trust needs the groups to enhance its public face. I would hate to see the two drift apart.

In my earlier Chapter 5 Bruce Abbott refers to the future development of Bletchley Park and the uncertainty of what shape and

In early April 2003, Tony Sale, left, explains the workings of the 'Colossus' computer rebuild in Bletchley Park to Bletchley's Andrew Meadley and a friend from Bristol, Nick Dodridge, right.

form this might take. Currently, and again as far as I am aware, the Trust has considered the selling for development of the area of the motor transport sheds and of H-block, the current home of Tony Sale's 'Colossus' rebuild and the original home of some of the ten 'Colossus' computers working in the Park during the war. I can understand, to some extent, the argument for not retaining the transport area, but I do feel strongly that the historic home of those 'Colossus' machines should stay. After all, the Trust's initial objective was to preserve ALL wartime buildings. Perhaps by the time these words are published, the position will be a little clearer, though all I can do here is to continue to wish the Trust, the support groups and anyone connected with the continuing struggle to keep Bletchley Park as a monument to that magnificent wartime work, the very best of luck in their endeavours. I will continue to do what I can. There is one last point about the Park that I would make, however, and it concerns a theory I have about F-block.

The only wartime buildings of stature to be demolished, and that was some years ago now, certainly before the Trust came into being, was F-block, which was itself home to 'Colossus' machines working on Japanese codes, among others. No-one seems to know why it was demolished, other than the work on razing it to the ground was arduous and took a long time because the block was so solidly built.

We do know, however, that Alan Turing made visits to the United States in the 1940s when the Americans were working on the building of the atomic bomb. With Turing being one of the world's top mathematicians, and 'Colossus' able to work out complex mathematical formulae, was the computer used to help the Americans in their work, and if so, was that why they pulled down F-block?

At a Trust gathering in the Park last year to unveil a memorial to the work of the early wartime Polish cryptographers, I was able to speak to a former senior member of staff at GCHQ, Cheltenham, who had said he wanted to meet me as chairman of the original Trust Steering Committee. We chatted awhile on matters general and then I put my theory to him. And he didn't say I was way off beam.

CHAPTER 8

PLANTS, BOWLS AND HORSES

Readers of the two earlier books in this series will know of my love of gardening and matters horticultural, instilled in me at an early age – though not then recognised – by my late father, who was an excellent grower of flowers and vegetables. What he wasn't interested in was fruit, other than the odd gooseberry bush, shrubs and lawns. Perverse it may seem, but the latter are all high on my gardening agenda now, though that is not to say I neglect vegetable and flower growing, as I hope later to explain.

Having moved to Edwin Close, Bow Brickhill, in 1967, Barbara, the children and I were faced with another large garden, though not quite the size we had at our previous home in the village, at The Pines, in Church Road. Edwin Close, though, was perhaps more of a challenge, for it was a brand new house and the plot on which it stood, though part of a former farmhouse garden, was an uncultivated area, with the garden space at the rear dominated by a small stand of young elm trees, about 15 feet high. The trees had no doubt seeded from the very tall elms that bordered the paddock which ran to one side of the garden and from which we had given the house its name – Tall Trees. But by the early 1970s not only had I grubbed out the young elms in the garden, but the older, taller trees were beginning to die, stricken with Dutch elm disease that decimated elms all over the country and changed the landscape completely. Thousands of elms throughout North Bucks had to be felled, as the branches just withered away with the complaint, caused by a particular form of beetle.

I laid a patio across the back of the house, complete with a small fishpond, put down a lawn, used shrubs and a few slow growing conifers to form a framework and then turned my attention to the L-shaped area outside the lawn and borders that I had purposely left. I planted a low privet hedge to define the L-shape more and within it planted a veg patch, a mini-orchard and some soft fruit. I still had room for a greenhouse and that came in time, where I tried my hand at growing melons, grapes and beneath the grape canopy, fuchsias. We were there from 1967–85 and I can only recall one major disaster – in an autumn gale in the late 1970s one of the poplar trees in the paddock next door came crashing down and took my greenhouse and its grape vines with it.

At the front of the house the garden was triangular, bordered on its two long sides by the drive and the farm barns in the paddock. I screened the walls of these barns with trellis covered in New Dawn climber roses, and put down a small lawn offset with a formal bed in which I usually grew tulips and wallflowers for an early display and a range of summer bedding later. But it was the space afforded by the back garden which was put to good use, with gatherings such as cheese and wine parties – barbecues were not fashionable at the time – or bring and buy sales for the Sports and Social Club.

For these Saturday summer evening events Peter Holland would provide a massive string of coloured lights which we would twine through the conifers and shrubs and next morning 'Sir Alf' – Ken Burton – would often appear to help me tidy up, the tidying up culminating in a pre-prandial glass or two sitting on a garden bench, surveying the lawn and invariably talking about the impending football season.

When we extended the house in 1983, as I have mentioned earlier, the patio was widened and I cut down on the veg patch to accommodate not one, but two greenhouses, the second inherited from my father after his death the year before. I turned one over to growing just fuchsias, while the other then boasted both grape vines and peaches. And some very good crops I had, too.

Moving to our present home in Bletchley in 1985 meant facing a tricky gardening problem, for not only were the front and back gardens smaller, but the back garden faced the wrong way. By that I mean it faces north and so gets not a lot of light until late in the day when the sun has moved to a more westerly aspect. The front garden is, of course, the opposite; it gets baked up. So in the front I now have to grow the sun lovers – lavenders, heathers, hebes, brooms – while at the back ferns, hostas, the fuchsias and other shrubs reign supreme. There is still room for a greenhouse, though, but minus grapes and peaches, for I need every bit of space now to bring on garden plants and to start off vegetables. And I grow vegetables by having extended my garden in one of the oldest of British ways. I have an allotment.

When I turned my back on working in London and joined Milton Keynes Development Corporation in 1989, I soon realised that I had created an extra 15 hours a week to call my own, simply by not having to sit on a train. So I got in touch with the Borough Council and was directed to the Windmill Hill Allotment site off Rosemullion Avenue, Tattenhoe, about a mile from home and where I took two plots, initially, on a 'buy one get one free' basis for the first year.

The reasonably secure site is fully serviced with water and toilet facilities, and has the additional benefit of being home to the trading hut of the Windmill Hill Garden and Allotment Association. Originally just calling itself an Allotment Association, the name was changed in 2000 when it was realised that many gardeners were under the impression that membership was purely for allotment holders.

The Association came into being at an inaugural meeting at the Windmill Hill Golf Club in April 1976, though in truth a temporary committee was in place earlier when Windmill Hill allotment holders got together to discuss the idea. However, the inaugural meeting put in place a formal mission statement which showed it to be a voluntary, non-profit making organisation which welcomed all gardeners, allotment holders or not.

Bulk buying for the benefit of members began almost immediately

The rear garden of Elmers Park in late Spring with the ornamental pool just in view in the foreground.

but the 'sales areas' by necessity were the members own garages and sheds. Realising something more substantial needed to be put in place, the committee set about erecting its first trading hut, a second hand unit, on a site on Windmill Hill Golf Club land in January 1978, with member John Ellis, an engineer, overseeing the operations. When the hut was relocated to the Tattenhoe allotment site in 1984, then extended in 1988, John was again at the forefront of operations. He served the Association in other ways too, being chairman from 1981–85 and treasurer from 1988–95. The current chairman is Peter Kendrew, having been elected to office in 1999, Roger Wyatt, who lives close to me in Church Green Road, is secretary and has been for more than ten years, and Janet Baxter has served as treasurer since 1995, taking over from John Ellis. Ted Lambert is the longest serving committee member, having been in office since 1977; the oldest Association member is 90-years-old Sam Mott, who is an honorary life member, the youngest 12-years-old Jake Brackley, who helps out at the trading hut at weekends. Other

Ready to serve two new customers at the Windmill Hill Garden and Allotment Association trading hut. Behind the counter, left to right, are Andrew Baxter, Jake Brackley, secretary Roger Wyatt, treasurer Janet Baxter and membership secretary Helen Vernon.

honorary life members include John Crippen, Ralph Vizard, who I know well as a fellow member of St Martin's Bowls Club, John Ellis, Bernard Warden and Jim Pringle.

The highlight of the trading year for the Association is in early February when gardeners from miles around descend on the hut over a weekend to buy their seed potatoes – many varieties are stocked – and onion sets ready for spring planting. Prices are way below what you would pay anywhere else. At its peak in 1988 the Association had 500 members with a waiting list, but, following the recession of that year, membership dipped slightly. The current membership stands at close to 400 with two dozen new members joining this season.

I find my allotment association friends, especially those who are fellow plot holders, an amiable and helpful bunch. We keep an eye on each other's plots, especially at holiday times, and I have been grateful on more than one occasion over the last dozen or so years for the can or two of water that has revived flagging beans or marrows while I've been away.

The windswept trio on a Sunday morning earlier this year on the Windmill Hill Allotment site are, left, Alpheus (Alf) Spencer, Ted Enever and right, Tony Pothecary. Alf has gardened on the site since 1982, Tony since 1984 and Ted since 1989. For the purist, the plant under inspection is 'Loch Ness', a thornless variety of blackberry.

I mentioned above Ralph Vizard, a fellow member of St Martin's Bowls Club, and that leads me to report that I took up 'the old man's game', as it is sometimes called, in the company of Jeremy West, one of my former Bow Brickhill football club team mates. I remember being disappointed when Jeremy told Ken Burton and me that he was hanging up his boots at a comparatively young age, but that he had decided at some stage in the future to try his hand at bowls. If ever I fancied it, he said, give him a shout. Well, Jeremy took up bowls by joining Woburn Sands Bowls Club, and in the early summer of 1985, I took up his invitation to give it a try. I enjoyed the challenge and joined the Woburn Sands club, believing that when we sold the Edwin Close house, then on the market, we would move to Woburn Sands where we had our eyes on several bungalows.

But it didn't turn out that way, for we moved to Bletchley instead in the October of that year, so, rather than travel all the way to Woburn Sands for a game of bowls, I opted to join St Martin's, whose green is only a short distance away in Rickley Park.

St Martin's is one of three bowls clubs in Bletchley, the other two being Bletchley Town, whose green is next door to the Leisure Centre, and Scot's, who have their green off Selbourne Avenue. St Martin's was formed in 1920 by men attending St Martin's church in Fenny Stratford and for many years its games were played on a green at the rear of St Martin's hall, in Queensway. In the early 1970s, however, the church commissioners sold off the land for development and St Martin's needed a new home. Rickley Park, serving Old and West Bletchley, was being laid down at the time and the new green became part of the Rickley Park complex, the club playing its first games there in 1975.

Now 83-years-old and still going strong, St Martin's has modern facilities by way of its clubhouse, bar, kitchen and changing rooms and often hosts county games. I played as much as I could while still working, served on the committee and sent in reports on games to the Citizen, but didn't make it to county playing standard, simply because I just never found the time to be practising as much as I should. But in 1996, and by then retired, I became club president, an office I held for three years.

I like to think that during that time I helped modernise the club to some extent. When I first took office, there was a great debate raging in bowls circles as to the rigidity of the dress code when playing games. Certainly it did seem to me to be a little old-fashioned, for I still don't know of any other outdoor game at the time which demanded that its men players wore ties. Now, as I have said in print before, I don't like ties, and it was maybe that little quirk that prompted me to write to the English Bowls Association (EBA) at its headquarters in Worthing, urging some modernisation. I'm glad to say that open-necked shirts are often now the norm and that shirts in club colours, instead of the formal plain white, are increasingly to be seen.

Though I could not comment on ladies' dress in my letter to the EBA, I knew that some lady players also felt constricted by the dress code. I also knew that at St Martin's, ladies were not allowed to vote at the AGM, even though there was a bona-fide ladies section at the club

The author, winner of the 2001 St Martin's Friday league cup.

and we often played 'mixed matches' – teams of both ladies and men – against other clubs. The club also relied heavily on its lady members to provide refreshments and carry out a range of other tasks, so it seemed to me only fitting within the day and age that they should be treated as equals. A special meeting in August 1998 threw out the inequality and from then on the ladies were able to vote at the AGM, as well as, I am pleased to say, the men taking on cleaning and refreshment duties. When I gave up office in 1999, Mavis Hickery, my vice president, took over to become St Martin's first lady president.

For the past couple of seasons I haven't played bowls at all, for putting the books together that make up this trilogy have taken much time and, dare I say, effort. Mavis had two years at the helm before handing over as president to Ken Meadley, who served the club for some years previously as secretary. Both Ken and his wife, Doris, are very keen bowlers and we see a lot of each other socially. Lorraine Hutchins is secretary and Stan Wickham is treasurer. Ken keeps on at me to get back on the green but I confess I usually reply with one of my favourite ripostes – that'll be the day! Still, an old war horse like me hasn't turned his back on bowls or other sports by a long way, as I will explain.

Once I had retired Barbara and Rachel made it clear that they would love to fulfill their ambition of going to Royal Ascot to see the horse-racing – and members of the Royal family, of course. So off we went, and it soon turned into an annual event. In 2001, stuck in a queue of traffic only a few miles from the course, we found ourselves behind a rather smart horsebox, obviously on its way to the races. I remember I made some quip about the horse inside having to be a pretty fast runner if it was to be in time for its race, and then thought no more about it. My daughter, Rachel, though, had other ideas. She had noticed the familiar www. written on the back doors of the horsebox and made a mental note. Later that evening, when we were back home, she called up the web address and found that the racing stables concerned, which were at Tring, offered a promotional video. A little later Rachel took a telephone call which invited the three of us there one morning for coffee.

We learned that the stables were owned and run by the successful trainer, Peter Harris, who firmly believes that racehorse ownership should be opened up to the ordinary man and woman. As such he has put together an ownership package not out of reach. All this was explained to us when we got there – and what a lovely place it is, set in 600 acres of Hertfordshire countryside. Briefly, Peter buys in yearlings at the major thoroughbred sales such as Newmarket and Doncaster. He assesses the horse's potential, works out a figure that will cover its cost to him, its training, veterinary and insurance and race fees over a two year period, and divides the end figure by twelve. He then sells the horse to a partnership of twelve people who become its registered owners after first choosing their name for the horse, the colours in which it will race, and the name of their partnership. For a one-off fee, which can be paid monthly, a member of a partnership gets two years racing from the horse. At the end of two years the horse is sold on, or fees to Peter can be renegotiated and he will keep it in training if that is the wish of the partnership. The stables has two yards, one for the two-year-olds at Pendley Farm, Tring, and one for the three-year-olds at Church Farm, Aldbury, just a mile up the road. Robert Eddery, the brother of former champion jockey, Pat, runs the two-year-old yard, while Jim Miller handles the three-year-olds at Aldbury.

Like all hobbies you tend to start on the bottom rung of the ladder and Rachel did just that, buying in to a pretty chestnut filly named Strudel Ruse within a few weeks of our visit. She was told that Strudel was never going to be the fastest thing in the world, but she came third in her first run at Brighton, which we were there to see. Owners, by the way, get two free tickets to the race meeting whenever their horse runs, all part of the Peter Harris package, and any winning monies are distributed to partnership members on a regular basis.

Strudel went on to run three more times but never improved; in truth she was a tiny filly and getting bumped by bigger colts in her races made her a bit apprehensive, I think. Peter's advice to the partnership was to sell her on after only one season, which they did, and she was retired from racing. But by this time, Rachel – and Mum and Dad – were enjoying the atmosphere of both racing stables and race meetings. The result was that we took a share in Sophrano, a bay colt who had his first run as a two-year-old at Lingfield in October 2002. He did extremely well to finish fifth and, two weeks later, we were at Yarmouth to see him improve by finishing third. As I write this, Barbara and Rachel have just returned from Church Farm where they watched him at work, and the word is he should be having his first run as a three-year-old very soon.

But it doesn't end there, for last November (2002) at Peter's annual parade of his yearlings, we took a chance on another bay colt, who has been named Baranook. Although only a year old this Spring, he is already classed as a two-year-old, for all racehorses have the same official birthday, the first of January. Because he is still very much a baby he is only in light training but, hopefully, he might well go out late in the season along the same lines as Sophrano.

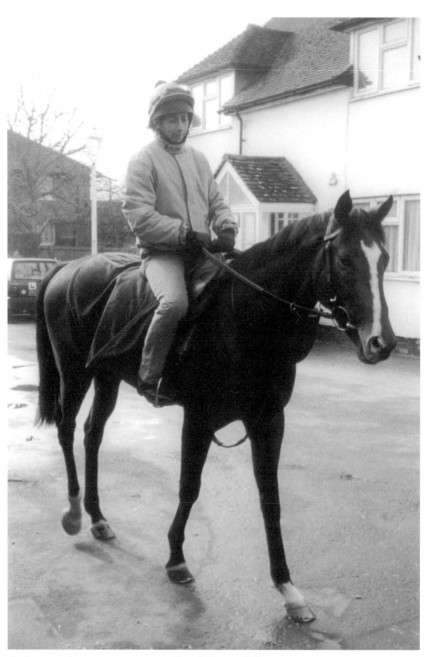

Sophrano on his way to exercise at Church Farm, Aldbury.

With Neil Callan up, Sophrano goes down to the seven furlong start at Yarmouth in October 2002 where he finished third. At the time of writing he is scheduled to run in a mile race at Kempton Park on 5 May 2003.

Baranook in November 2002 at the yearling parade at Pendley Farm, Tring.

So, if any reader wants to experience the thrills of the sport of kings, I can thoroughly recommend getting in touch with Peter Harris Racing at Tring. As an owner the stables are open to you seven days a week, there are special events there throughout the year, and, who knows, the Enevers could yet be leading in a Derby winner! Alright; say it: That'll be the day!

So, as I complete the task of producing the various chapters, illustrations and captions that will go to make up this book, it is Spring 2003 and I will be 69 years old in August. By the following month, September, I will have spent 63 of those 69 years living in the Woburn Sands and Bletchley districts.

The physical and social changes that those of my age group have witnessed during those years have been phenomenal, with the arrival and development of the new city of Milton Keynes being the most pronounced. There is no doubt in my mind now, though doubts were certainly there nearly 40 years ago when the new city was first mooted, that Milton Keynes is, by and large, a well planned conurbation.

Over the years it has offered, and continues to offer, career opportunities to many and a lifestyle to be envied by those living in Britain's older towns and cities. But this is not to say that Milton Keynes is some magic sort of Utopia — you only have to look at the problems facing Bletchley that I have highlighted in this book to realise that. And, of course, we all suffer from the trials and tribulations that affect us on a national basis. Poor and unreliable public transport, long waiting lists for hospital treatment, the education of our children ever in some sort of turmoil, the problems of asylum seekers, for we have surely lost control of our own borders, and above all, a judicial system which is now nothing more than a joke. Some of the things that happen in this area of everyday life you couldn't make up and if they weren't so serious, would be hilarious. How else can you describe the actions of a serial burglar who tries to sue his victim, who injured him, for loss of earnings? I refer, of course, to the Tony Martin case, the Norfolk farmer in jail for manslaughter and whose parole was recently turned down because he told the authorities he felt safer from crime in 1952 than he did in the 1990s. His parole assessors said he was living in the past. I've learned only today, though, that Tony Martin has been given leave to appeal, and I wish him luck.

Now I confess I hold no political allegiance, and have not done so since the 1970s when I resigned from the Conservative party when Mrs Thatcher took away free milk for children at school and tried to impose fees on rural families whose children were taken to school by bus. So what I would love to see is the formation of a new political party called 'The Common Sense' party. I don't suppose for one minute that would cure all our ills, but if it brought some common sense to the judiciary and education sectors alone it would be a good start. And if it made sure lottery monies went to good causes in this country, rather than to obscure projects such as fattening guinea pigs in South America – yes, that is a fact – then that would be another common sense step. As my old Mum would have said in a case like that: 'Charity begins at home!'

But there, am I now talking common sense, or are they just the musings of a Victor Meldrew-type, seeing evil in things not being as they were many years ago. I don't think so, but then again, my common sense may not be your common sense. So, the dream of a common sense political party? Only one thing to say as I bring this overview of our little corner of North Bucks to an end.

That'll be the day!

COCKNEY KID AND COUNTRYMEN
**The Second World War remembered by the children
of Woburn Sands and Aspley Guise**

Ted Enever

On the evening of Saturday 7th September 1940, London's East End lay under a pall of smoke from heavy bombing by the German Luftwaffe. It was the beginning of what history was to record as the Blitz.

Six year old Ted and his parents were victims of that first attack. With home and possessions lost, they left London to find safety, shelter and a new way of life in the villages of Woburn Sands and Aspley Guise.

"Cockney Kid and Countrymen" is Ted Enever's story of that new way of life and a snapshot of the wartime years vividly remembered by the village children of the time.

Ted was educated at Bedford Modern School and entered journalism in 1951 with the Bletchley District Gazette. After two years national service he continued his career as a freelance journalist, with various large organisations. On retirement he was working for Milton Keynes Development Corporation. A founder member of the Bletchley Park Trust and now a Patron, Ted is author of "Britains Best Kept Secret – Ultra's base at Bletchley Park."

160

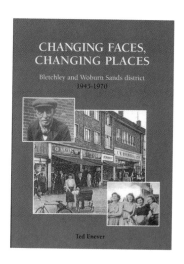

CHANGING FACES, CHANGING PLACES
Bletchley and Woburn Sands district
1945–1970

Ted Enever

'Changing Faces, Changing Places' looks at the 25 year period between the end of the Second World War and the decision to build the new city of Milton Keynes. What occurred then was to turn that part of North Bucks from a collection of small towns and rural villages into the fastest growing urban development in western Europe.

Drawing on the recollections of a wide range of local people, 'Changing Faces, Changing Places' is a sequel to Ted Enever's successful 'Cockney Kid and Countrymen'. From his days travelling by train to Bedford Modern School and through various jobs, particularly as journalist and editor on several local newspapers, it continues the author's own story of life in Aspley Guise, Woburn Sands, Bow Brickhill and Bletchley, told in his own distinctive style.

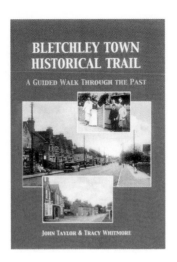

BLETCHLEY TOWN HISTORICAL TRAIL
A guided walk through the past

John Taylor and Tracy Whitmore

Using a fascinating dual approach, The 'Bletchley Trail' offers a nostalgic walk in search of bygone Bletchley (including Fenny Stratford and Water Eaton), accompanied by historical revelations about many of the town's prominent buildings.

The 'Bletchley Trail' takes the reader from one end of the town to the other, stopping at dozens of landmarks to reveal their history, whilst recounting key episodes and unusual events.

Illustrated with a wealth of rare photographs, the book is therefore an ideal introduction to the history of Bletchley as well as providing the perfect companion to a unique tour of the town.

BUCKINGHAM AT WAR

Pip Brimson

The people of Buckingham adapted well to a state of war. Their stories reflect courage, humour and occasional pathos.

How they coped with A.R.P., gas masks, blackout, mobilization and the secrets of Bletchley Park, followed by the formation of the Home Guard, Land Girls, and the jobs women were directed to. The progress of the war through those early years, which included rationing and evacuation, individual efforts by those at home and fund raising events in the town are all related in this book. The collection of salvage took a large part – as did the knitting of comforts for the Forces by local women's groups. Everything was geared for eventual Victory, however long it might take.

When at last the end of the War approached, the blackout was lifted; the Home Guard, their job finished, stood down, and prisoners of war overseas began to return home to great rejoicing, which culminated on V.E. and V.J. Days. Servicemen too, were slowly beginning to demobilize.

Finally, everyone could sit back and take stock – attend to their losses and sadness, but feel proud of what had been achieved – and then, begin to prepare for the problems and happiness Peace would bring, after long years of struggle and endeavour.

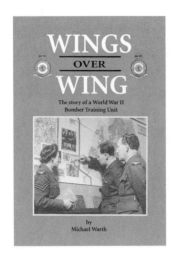

**WINGS OVER WING
The Story of a World War 11 Bomber
Training Unit**

Michael Warth

For five years at the beginning of the 1940s the quiet countryside around the Buckinghamshire village of Wing was the scene of a period of activity not witnessed in those parts before or since. It was then that an area of flat agricultural land was converted into an airfield and utilized by the Royal Air Force for training of bomber aircrew.

The peaceful country lanes were soon busy with the movement of men, women and vehicles whilst the skies above were filled with Wellington bombers and many other types of aircraft as they took off and landed at RAF Wing.

Events at the airfield, and those involving Number 26 Operational Training Unit which was based there, touched the lives of many as hundreds of trainee pilots, navigators, bomb aimers and gunners embarked on a ten week training course, before moving on to their respective squadrons.

There are stories of great courage and comradeship, where trust and faith in each other was paramount as well as stories of great sadness because such ties were too often tragically broken by the ravages of war.

"Wings Over Wing" is an attempt to reconstruct events at just one of a number of bomber training units. The stories recounted by 'those who were there' are backed up by factual records and documents and augmented by photographs and illustrations with the aim of giving some insight into life at such an establishment in the extraordinary days of World War 11.

DEADLY DEEDS
A compilation of Buckinghamshire murder cases

Len Woodley

Included in this book are accounts of fourteen murders that have occurred within the County of Buckingham, plus one from central Europe. You will read about the Victorian 'Quaker' who, having escaped the gallows once, faced them again some years later; the country squire killed walking home from church; the gypsy who robbed and killed an old man, and the husband who shot his wife and her lover in one county, was tried in another and executed in yet another. A domestic dispute that went horribly wrong; a doctor murdered whilst out with her dog on an afternoon stroll and a Policeman who caught a killer as he patrolled his beat. A man who was killed in an argument over a dog; a teenager murdered by someone she thought she could trust and a young woman killed by an itinerant she had befriended. A Greenham Common woman, who accepted a lift in a car and was murdered because she did so and a young mother killed by a youth she allowed into her house.

The author was a Police officer for thirty years, serving in both uniform and C.I.D.

HISTORIC FIGURES
IN THE BUCKINGHAMSHIRE LANDSCAPE

John Houghton

For centuries the County of Buckinghamshire has evolved, remaining always pastoral and agricultural. Yet, in terms of national history, Bucks has been no backwater. It has played its part in times of national crisis and upheaval. It has furnished great leaders, whether in politics or in art. It is rich in 'cards and characters' whose eccentricity excites interest. Like any other county, it has its heroes and villains.

The book tells of 100 "figures in a Buckinghamshire landscape". They include: warriors and men-at-arms, statesmen and politicians, literary geniuses, polemicists and agitators, plutocrats and tycoons, plotters and regicides and some ordinary folk who did ordinary things! These 100 individuals were as diverse as could be. What links them all is that Bucks was their county, either by birth or by adoption.

In the final chapter there are a further 12,000 "figures in a Buckinghamshire landscape" – they are the Code Breakers of Bletchley Park.

CHILTERN WALKS
Buckinghamshire

Nick Moon

One in a series of three books providing a comprehensive coverage of walks throughout the whole of the Chiltern area (as defined by the Chiltern Society). The walks included vary in length from 3.0 to 10.9 miles, but are mainly in the 5–7 mile range popular for half-day walks, although suggestions of possible combinations of walks are given for those preferring a full day's walk.

Each walk gives details of nearby places of interest and is accompanied by a specially drawn map of the route which also indicates local pubs and a skeleton road network.

167

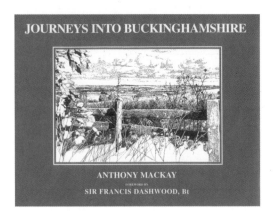

JOURNEYS INTO BUCKINGHAMSHIRE

Anthony Mackay

One in a series of three books of ink drawings revealing an intriguing historic heritage and capturing the spirit of England's rural heartland, ranging widely over cottages and stately homes, over bridges, churches and mills, over sandy woods, chalk downs and watery river valleys.

Every corner of Buckinghamshire has been explored in the search for material, and, although the choice of subjects is essentially a personal one, the resulting collection represents a unique record of the environment today.

The notes and maps, which accompany the drawings, lend depth to the books, and will assist others on their own journeys around the counties.

Anthony Mackay's pen-and-ink drawings are of outstanding quality. An architectural graduate, he is equally at home depicting landscapes and buildings. The medium he uses is better able to show both depth and detail than any photograph.